Wiley Keys to Success

How to Ace Any Test

Beverly Ann Chin is Professor of English, Director of the English Teaching Program, former Director of the Montana Writing Project, and a former President of the National Council of Teachers of English.

Dr. Chin is a nationally recognized leader in English language arts standards, curriculum instruction, and assessment. Many schools and states call upon her to help them develop programs in reading and writing across the curriculum. Dr. Chin has edited and written numerous books and articles in the field of English language arts. She is the author of *On Your Own: Writing* and *On Your Own: Grammar*.

Wiley Keys to Success

HOW TO ACE ANY TEST

Beverly Ann Chin, Ph.D.
Series Consultant

WILEY

John Wiley & Sons, Inc.

Developed, Designed and Produced by BOOK BUILDERS LLC

Published by John Wiley & Sons, Inc., Hoboken, New Jersey
Published simultaneously in Canada

For general information about our other products and services, please contact our Customer Care Department within the United States at (800) 762-2974, outside the United States at (317) 572-3993 or fax (317) 572-4002.

Wiley also publishes its books in a variety of electronic formats. Some content that appears in print may not be available in electronic books. For more information about Wiley products, visit our web site at www.wiley.com.

Library of Congress Cataloging-in-Publication Data:

How to ace any test. / Beverly Ann Chin, series consultant.
  p. cm.
  Includes index.
  ISBN 0-471-43156-7 (pkb. : alk. paper)
  1. Examinations—Study guides—Juvenile literature. 2. Educational tests and measurements—Study guides—Juvenile literature. 3. Test-taking skills—Juvenile literature.
  LB3051.H843 2004
373.126—dc22   2004002223

10 9 8 7 6 5 4 3 2 1

DEAR STUDENTS

Welcome to the **WILEY KEYS TO SUCCESS** series! The books in this series are practical guides designed to help you be a better student. Each book focuses on an important area of schoolwork, including building your vocabulary, studying and doing homework, writing research papers, taking tests, and more.

Each book contains seven chapters—the keys to helping you improve your skills as a student. As you understand and use each key, you'll find that you will enjoy learning more than ever before. As a result, you'll feel more confident in your classes and be better prepared to demonstrate your knowledge.

I invite you to use the **WILEY KEYS TO SUCCESS** series at school and at home. As you apply each key, you will open the doors to success in school as well as to many other areas of your life. Good luck, and enjoy the journey!

Beverly Ann Chin, Series Consultant
Professor of English
University of Montana, Missoula

NOTE TO TEACHERS, LIBRARIANS, AND PARENTS

The **WILEY KEYS TO SUCCESS** series is a series of handbooks designed to help students improve their academic performance. Happily, the keys can open doors for everyone—at home, in school, at work.

Each book is an invaluable resource that offers seven simple, practical steps to mastering an important aspect of schoolwork, such as building vocabulary, studying and doing homework, taking tests, and writing research papers. We hand readers seven keys—or chapters—that show them how to increase their success as learners—a plan intended to build lifelong learning skills. Reader-friendly graphics, self-assessment questions, and comprehensive appendices provide additional information.

Helpful features scattered throughout the books include "Writing it Right," which expands on the text with charts, graphs, and models; "Inside Secret," which reveals all-important hints, rules, definitions, and even warnings; and "Ready, Set, Review," which makes it easy for students to remember key points.

WILEY KEYS TO SUCCESS *are designed to ensure that all students have the opportunity to experience success.* Once students know achievement, they are more likely to become independent learners, effective communicators, and critical thinkers. Many readers will want to use each guidebook by beginning with the first key and progressing systematically to the last key. Some readers will select the keys they need most and integrate what they learn with their own routines.

As educators and parents, you can encourage students to use the books in this series to assess their own strengths and weaknesses as learners. Using students' responses and your own observations of their study skills and habits, you can help students develop positive attitudes, set realistic goals, form successful schedules, organize materials, and monitor their own academic progress. In addition, you can discuss how adults use similar study strategies and communication skills in their personal and professional lives.

We hope you and your students will enjoy the **WILEY KEYS TO SUCCESS** series. We think readers will turn to these resources time and time again. By showing students how to achieve everyday success, we help children grow into responsible, independent young adults who value their education—and into adults who value learning throughout their lives.

Beverly Ann Chin, Series Consultant
Professor of English
University of Montana, Missoula

CONTENTS

Introduction

Tests—Do We Need Them?

A test is coming into your life. It may be next month, or it may be next Tuesday. It might even be tomorrow! How will you do?

You might feel completely prepared, and ready to take on the toughest questions. Or you may worry that you'll get so nervous, you can't come up with any answers. Suppose you stayed up all night trying to cram? You might be so tired, you'd fall asleep right on the test paper. What if you find questions about things you've never heard of? Or worse, suppose you almost know the answers. If only you'd studied a little harder, or took better notes in class. What if your head explodes from trying to fill it with too many facts?

Maybe that's going a little too far. The truth is that although very few people seem to enjoy taking tests, they can actually do better on them if they try to make them a little bit fun. When you think of taking a test, try to picture yourself as a guest on a game show. Or try to compete with yourself to do better on each new test than you did on the last one. Taking a test involves more than just answering specific questions to give you a certain number of points to pass a course.

Tests are not punishment. They give you and your teacher feedback on how much you are learning. They let you know whether you've misunderstood an important concept or whether you should work harder in a certain subject. They also can show where you're doing especially well.

Taking tests is a skill in its own right—and one that you'll use throughout your life. As you move on in school, tests may help you decide whether to take an advanced class. If your heart is set on going to a special high school, you'll want to do your best on the type of test that will help you get admitted. Of course, tests also are a big part of getting into college. In college, doing well on tests in certain subjects can even help you skip those courses!

When it comes to getting certain types of jobs, taking a test is part of that too. Do you want to become a police officer or fire fighter, a real estate agent or an accountant? At some point—you guessed it!—you'll need to pass a test. Lots of other jobs depend on tests, too.

Aside from those types of tests, think about the kinds of tests you take to help you in other parts of life, such as a driver's test, a first-aid test, and a swimming test. Tests are definitely a part of life, so learning to do your best when taking them can make life a little easier. And just think how easy it can be if you learn to *enjoy* taking tests!

What you need is a plan—something better than hoping you get the flu on test day. This book can help you make that plan. Its tips and hints will help you remember what you've learned in class. You'll discover strategies on how to take a test efficiently. If you follow the seven keys to success, you're sure to ace any test that comes your way.

BE PREPARED

✓ **Forming Good Habits**

✓ **Asking Questions**

✓ **Finding Out What You Need to Know**

✓ **Studying for Different Kinds of Tests**

When it comes to taking a test, it doesn't matter how many pages you read or how many hours you spend staring at your notes—if you don't know how to prepare yourself for success.

When a football player scores a touchdown or a dancer hits all the right moves in a routine, they have prepared themselves by understanding the keys to success. Before you can do well on a test, you have to form good habits, ask the right questions, and find out what you need to know. After learning what kind of

test you'll be taking, you will be prepared to practice the skills needed for your own winning score.

Forming Good Habits

Being a good student doesn't take magic. You'll find studying gets easier when you have a positive attitude, stay organized, and feel ready and willing to work. What can you do to make sure you're on the right path to forming good habits? Make sure to pay attention in class, take good notes, ask questions, do your homework, and review regularly. (For more detailed tips on effective study habits, read the Wiley Keys to Success Series book, *How to Study for Success.*)

Pay attention and take notes in class

Paying attention in class seems like an obvious habit of good students. When you pay attention, you also should be thinking about what is important to remember and write down. Your teacher can say a lot during a class, but you don't want to take down every word your teacher says. A good note-taker is like a detective. Watch your teacher for clues about what topics are important. Does your teacher write on the board? That's probably a major topic. Is some information mentioned several times? Start writing in your notebook. Does the teacher hand out a sheet about the topic while discussing it? Does the topic appear on the overhead projector? Better get it down!

Now you have important information to put in your notebook. How do you write it down? Do you just scribble everything together? That makes important points hard to find at review time. Organizing your notes can help you study later. When something goes up on the board, use that for a heading. When your teacher makes a point, give that fact its own special line. Leave plenty of space between these points—then you can add your own notes and comments. Underline important phrases.

Some students think of their class notes as a first draft. After class they recopy what they scribbled down. This does more than make their notes neat and simpler to study. Rewriting in your own words can help you remember facts better. If you take clear notes and make mental connections as you listen, you'll have an easier time when it comes to reviewing for tests.

Do your homework

When you do your homework consistently, you also are preparing for tests. You're reading up on and answering questions about what you learned in class. Often, homework shows the kinds of questions that might turn up on tests. Also, when homework is graded, you get a chance to find out what kind of answers your teacher prefers.

Good homework doesn't get done quickly. Good students learn *time management*, how to put their time to the best use. Suppose you end up with free time at school. Why not use it to tackle homework? For example, you could complete a reading assignment if the weather keeps you in for recess.

If you have after-school activities, hitting the books *before* you go to practice helps you make sure the schoolwork gets done. By using those often wasted minutes between school and late afternoon activities for homework, you may be surprised to find how much more time you've made for doing other, fun things in the evening.

Once you're aware of *when* to do your homework, it helps to know *where* to do it. It's important to avoid distractions when doing homework and studying for tests. Some people may say that music or TV "relaxes" them, but imagine they're taking an important test. Would they really want their favorite songs or TV programs on to take their minds off their work? The answer, of course, is "No." Everyone works better without distractions.

KEY 1

If it's a big job, break it into easy pieces

Sometimes, you may look at your homework list and not know where to start. Does this look like a typical day of assignments from your school?

Language Arts:
20 spelling words
10 vocabulary words to define
and use in a sentence.
Read the next three chapters
in the class novel

Math:
3 examples and 10 word problems
Science:
A sheet with an experiment to
do and then write about
Social Studies:
A reading assignment with
5 questions to answer

A research paper about
a neighboring state

First, tackle the things that are due tomorrow while you're fresh and sharp. Next, work on a certain amount of a future assignment—for instance, the first five words in both the spelling and vocabulary lists. If you need to set something up for the science experiment, do that. Maybe you should let your parents know that you need some special materials. Then, you might want to look through a book or explore the state's website on the Internet to find preliminary information for your research paper. Finally, you might read a chapter in the novel. With any luck, you'll still have time for your favorite TV show.

Making a schedule that allows you to do a little at a time helps shrink big jobs down into smaller ones. Some jobs, like memorizing, actually happen easily if you work in small bits. Five ten-minute memorizing sessions spread over a week help you remember more information than you would if you crammed lots of facts into one hour of study time in one evening. If you keep putting off the work, you may find yourself facing too much to do all at once. One night isn't enough to write a research paper, do a science experiment, finish regular homework, and study for a spelling test. Something is going to suffer, and so will you. However, if you do a part of each project every day—who knows? You might even finish your research paper or science experiment *before* it's due.

Asking Questions

Have you heard this old saying: "How will I know if I don't ask?" That's twice as important when you're in school. If you don't understand something, ask about it. You're not the only one who'll learn. Other students benefit, too. No matter how much your classmates might groan, lots of kids may feel just as lost as you do. Plus, your teacher may see that this topic needs more work. Everyone can feel better about discovering a problem in a class discussion rather than on a test.

Don't be shy. Speak up, and try to make sure your questions are clear. Just saying, "I don't get this!" doesn't help anyone. Instead, you might ask, "I don't understand why we use the words, 'Everybody knows.' Isn't 'everybody' a lot of people? Shouldn't it take a plural verb?" Now you're asking about something specific.

Keep in mind that while teachers want to answer your questions, they also want to cover a certain amount of material in each class session. If you have a lot of questions, you may want to save them for after class. Also, if you feel embarrassed about asking for help, you might find it easier to talk to your teacher privately. No teacher wants to see a student fail. Talking helps both of you do your jobs better—

GETTING IT RIGHT

Questions to Ask

Remember that a good question gives the teacher a launching pad to discuss problems. Here are some ways to ask questions that teachers will appreciate:

"I'm not sure I understand this writing assignment. Could you explain exactly what you need?"

"Could you give us a hint on Problem 19?"

Or, even better, "Could you show us how to set up Problem 31?"

"I'm having a hard time with this part of the chapter. What does the author mean when she says, 'Love doesn't sit like a stone, it always has to be made new, like bread'?"

Bring up a math problem you didn't get right. "This is how I tried to work it out. Could you show me where I went wrong?"

If you have a Social Studies report that isn't going well, ask "How can I expand my ideas? Can you show me what I'm missing?"

learning and teaching. Even if you're not doing well in a class, asking questions shows that you're trying.

If you don't have time to talk after class, write your question down and put it on the teacher's desk. The teacher may give you an answer later or give the whole class a review on the topic. Most importantly, when a teacher gives you help, *write the information down.* When the time comes to review the trouble spot, you'll have the explanation that clears it up right there in front of you.

Review every day

People are always on the run these days. Homework, activities, life in general can make you feel that you have no time at all. Why should you take time to sit down with your notebook and reread what you already wrote down? For one thing, you get a chance to fill in any words or ideas you might have missed while your teacher's words are still fresh in your mind. (Now you can see why it's a good idea to leave lots of space as you write notes in class.)

Daily reviews also help you remember the day's work. Experiments have shown that people begin to forget information within 24 hours. The more material you hold onto, the easier time you'll have studying for tests. Rereading your notes helps the information stay in your mind. In fact, the more often you see this information, the more likely you are to remember it.

Be critical as you read your notes. Do you understand what's written there? If not, check your textbook. Still confused? Write some questions for the next class. Even when your notes make sense, you can still add comments from what you read in your textbook. That way, your notes are clearer when you go back to study them next time.

Finding Out What You Need to Know

As test time comes closer, you must concentrate on learning what you *need* to learn. Many students do this by continually asking, "Will this be on the test?" Teachers hear this question over and over again, year after year, and have learned how to avoid simply giving you the answer on a silver platter. You do have other ways to get the information, however. Here are some helpful hints on how to get some helpful hints.

What will the test cover?

While teachers don't hand out the questions and answers for an upcoming test, they do give clues. You already know to pay attention in class. In the days before the test, listen especially carefully to what your teacher has to say. What points does he or she stress or repeat in class? Are any of them different from topics in your textbook? You may want to ask your teacher whether this is important information that was overlooked in the text, or whether it is not as crucial as information that's taught in the book. This is another way of asking, "Will this be on the test?"

Many teachers set aside class time for a pre-test review. Keep your eyes and ears open during these run-throughs. They're a gold mine of test information! Sometimes a teacher may schedule a special study session during lunch or after school. Join the group and pay special attention to anything you don't already know. Some teachers hand out study guides or worksheets with review material. Read them carefully. Are you comfortable with all the topics? If you spot unfamiliar information, ask about it so you can avoid any surprises during test time.

If the teacher doesn't review before the test, then go over your class notes carefully. Make a list of every topic you consider important. Skim through the textbook chapters and do the same thing. Pay special attention to headings within the chapters. Compare these two lists and combine them. Before the test, find a chance to show this super-list to the teacher. Ask if these topics cover what's important for the test. Listen carefully. If the teacher suggests additional topics, write them down! If they seem totally unfamiliar, ask where you can get more information. You still have time to study them.

Studying for Different Kinds of Tests

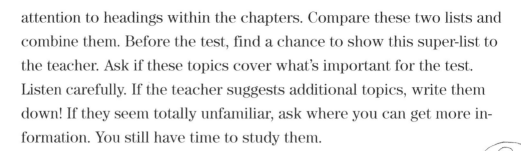

Almost as important as knowing the answers is understanding the questions. What types of questions will be on the test? Will you find matching columns, fill-in-the-blanks, multiple-choice questions? Will you have to write essays?

Your study plans may change depending on the kinds of questions you'll face. Short-answer questions demand that you know lots of facts. You must fill your memory with names and dates, parts of speech, or math formulas. Writing essays demands a broad grasp of a subject. You must know how different topics, events, or ideas come together.

Often, tests mix both kinds of questions. So you'll have to fine-tune your studying style. If you memorize only facts, dates, and names, will you know how to tie them together to answer an essay question? If you concentrate on "the big picture" to cover the essay, will you know all the supporting details needed to answer the shorter questions?

There are no correct answers to these questions—you have to find the balance that's right for you. If you have a hard time memorizing, at least 60 percent of your time (and maybe more) should go into studying the short answers. If essays are a challenge for you, spend more time preparing for them.

What if it's a standardized test?

More and more states have begun tracking how students and schools are doing with standardized tests. These exams test what students have learned in their past several years in school. For instance, tests might be given in the fourth and then the eighth grades. The scores can affect the jobs of teachers and principals, the amount of money that goes to running a school, and the requirements a student may need to meet in order to graduate with the rest of his or her class.

Mostly, these tests feature multiple-choice questions, which are answered by filling in a special test form, often called *bubble forms* because you mark your answers in small circles that cover the page. Getting familiar with the style of the questions and practicing the correct way to answer them is an important part of what you need to study when preparing for these tests. You can find sample questions for standardized tests in Appendix A at the end of this book.

How long will it be?

The longer the advance notice you receive about a test, the bigger it is likely to be. A pop quiz may only have five questions and take fifteen minutes. A final exam may go on for several hours. The quiz might cover only last night's reading, while the final reviews your whole year's work. Knowing when a test is coming allows you to plan your preparation well ahead of time. Here's a quick rule to remember: the longer the test, the more time you'll need to study for it.

When the test actually comes, you'll also have to consider how much time you have in which to finish the test. Whether you have fifteen minutes or two hours, remember to pace yourself. Often, doing well means matching the right test-taking strategy to the amount of time available. You'll learn more about test-taking strategies later in this book. For now, start by focusing on what it takes to become the best student you can be.

Ready, Set, *REVIEW*

1. Many students complain about how much time they spend on homework. How much time are you spending? For the next week, take a sheet of notebook paper and jot down the times when you begin and end homework sessions. If you have to break off to go somewhere or to eat dinner, subtract the time when you're not doing homework.

   After a week has gone by, you'll have a rough idea of how much of your day goes into doing homework. In the next exercise, you can put that information to good use.

2. On another sheet of notebook paper, make a chart breaking down the time from when you get home from school until you go to bed. Each line can represent fifteen minutes. If you get home at 3 p.m., write that on the first line. The next line reads 3:15, the one after that 3:30, and so on. Now comes the hard part. Use an alarm clock or kitchen timer to keep track of what you are doing during each of these fifteen-minute periods. Write down *exactly* what you were doing during each of them. Were you eating a snack, listening to music, catching a glimpse of what was on TV, talking on the phone, or daydreaming? Or were you doing homework?

   After filling out this chart for three days, you'll have a better picture of how you use your homework time. How many minutes did you actually spend working? How many minutes did you put into other things? If you find blocks of wasted time, think of ways to eliminate them. Maybe you need a schedule. You might get more done by breaking your hour into fifty minutes of working time with a ten-minute break than just taking short breaks whenever you feel like it. After all, four short breaks of five minutes each end up taking twenty minutes out of your study or homework time.

PRACTICE, PRACTICE, PRACTICE

✓ **Prepare to Study**

✓ **Budget Your Time**

✓ **Identify Key Concepts and Facts**

✓ **Basic Study Tools**

✓ **Study Groups**

> *You know the old saying: "Practice makes perfect." Becoming good at anything takes work.*

However good you might be at something, you get better when you practice. To win computer games, you have to learn some tricks and get into the habit of using them. The same thing is true if you're into music: You have to practice if you want to play a guitar well or improve your singing.

With practice, you can teach your brain to remember information for tests, too. Sometimes, the job requires memorizing. It's the only way to remember multiplication tables, spelling words, names and dates, and phone numbers. With other types of information, you have to remember what's important about the connections between different ideas. By learning how to be a good student, you'll understand more about what's important to study and how to focus on that. And you'll increase your ability to do well on every test you take.

Succeeding at tests is all about what you *remember*. Only recently scientists have been able to map where memory takes place in the brain. They've also identified three ways of remembering: *short-term memory*, which fades away quickly; *working memory*, which fades less quickly; and *long-term memory*, which can stay around for life. Look at it this way: When you cross a street, your short-term memory keeps track of traffic. You don't really need to remember which cars were where after you're safely across, so you quickly forget that information. Working memory remembers why you crossed the street—for example, to visit a store. Two weeks later, you might have a hard time recalling which store you went to and what you bought there. Long-term memory holds onto things you always need to remember, like how to read.

When you read a textbook, review your notes, or listen to a class discussion, the information goes into your short-term memory. Unless you do something to help you remember it better, it could fade away by test time. By studying, your goal is to move information into long-term memory—or at least working memory that lasts until the test—so here's how to how to study for long-term success. (You can turn to Appendix C at the end of this book for a list of "Top Ten Tips for Remembering What You Studied.")

Prepare to Study

The way to ace any test is to come prepared. Depending on how important the test is, clear your schedule for a week or even two because now is the time to hit the books.

The Perfect Study Space

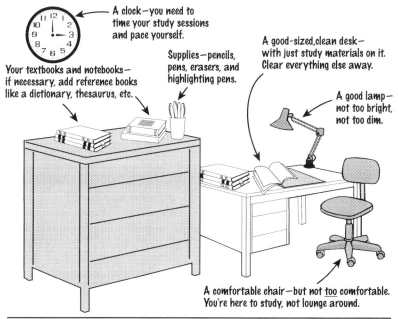

A clock—you need to time your study sessions and pace yourself.

Your textbooks and notebooks— if necessary, add reference books like a dictionary, thesaurus, etc.

Supplies—pencils, pens, erasers, and highlighting pens.

A good-sized, clean desk— with just study materials on it. Clear everything else away.

A good lamp— not too bright, not too dim.

A comfortable chair—but not <u>too</u> comfortable. You're here to study, not lounge around.

Distractions to avoid!

KEEP OFF

Plan your study time for when you're feeling most alert. Also, don't try to do something else at the same time. Research shows that students do best when they always study in the same place.

Budget Your Time

This part of the studying job is where your clock comes in. If you have several tests to prepare for, decide how much time you need to spend on each subject. Then break down that time. Schedule tough ideas or subjects for when you're most awake and alert.

Do you tend to put things off? Then in the beginning start your study time with easier material that you enjoy—at least until you get into the swing of studying. As you build better study habits and learn to get to work more quickly, try to start with the tough stuff first and then "reward" yourself by moving on to a favorite or easier subject.

How long should you study? Try to break your sessions into one-hour blocks, which include 50 minutes of study time and a 10-minute break. (You may need more frequent breaks as you start out.) A long, straight 50 minutes is good for organizing concepts, noting relationships, or writing summaries of your notes. Use shorter, 15-minute time blocks for memorizing,

INSIDE SECRET

"Feed" Your Brain

Watching what you eat can help you study! Make sure you get three good meals a day. and think healthy when you eat snacks on your study breaks. A piece of fruit is a better choice than a bowl of Sugar Buzz Bombs.

revising notes, or answering practice questions. When you find yourself growing bored or getting tired, make a change. Switch the job you're doing or go to a new subject. To create a helpful schedule for putting your study time to its best use, turn to Appendix B at the end of this book.

How should you spend a break? Get up from your desk. Walk around a bit. Stretch. Maybe have a light snack to help boost your energy. (Just remember, it's a snack, not a four-course meal.)

Identify Key Concepts and Facts

Ask any student about getting ready for a test, and you're sure to hear: "There's so much to study!" Remember, though, you're not being tested on every word in the textbook or even every word said in class. Some material is more important.

Your first job is to identify what really counts. Look at your class notes. What did your teacher spend a long time discussing? Was there a review session in class for the upcoming test? What did the teacher emphasize?

Look in your textbook. What topics are stressed there? One way to spot important points is to check each chapter heading, each subheading within the chapters, and boldface words. Check the questions at the end of each chapter. These show what the textbook author thought was important. If your textbook has an index, check which topics turn up on a lot of pages.

For major exams, you can also get a hint of what your teacher thinks is important if you save and review old tests throughout the year. What questions appeared on tests as the class started off? What was asked on the midterm? If topics were important then, they're likely to pop up on a final exam.

As you identify important topics, make a list of them. Write a brief summary about each point on your list. Pay careful attention as you work. The process of writing is important for memory. In fact, research shows that writing things down actually helps you remember them.

Basic Study Tools

In Key 3, you'll see how different kinds of questions need different kinds of practice. However, you can use the following tools to help you learn the basics about any subject you study.

Single-answer questions

The best thing about single-answer questions is . . . they're short. The worst thing is that they're based on hundreds, maybe thousands, of little facts. How are you supposed to nail down all those answers? It takes a lot of work, mainly memorizing, but here are some ways to make the job easier.

Make your own flashcards. The smartest strategy is to start making flashcards from the first day of class. Each time you come across an important date, event, person, or definition, make a flashcard. Practice with them. As you collect more and more answers, divide the cards into two piles: "What I know" and "What I don't know." As test time comes up, flashcard practice becomes review more than learning. Close to test time, be sure to go through your whole pile and refresh your memory.

Underlining and highlighting. You can underline or highlight important facts or definitions in your notebook when you review your notes after class. That way, your eye jumps to that item.

Keep it short. Keep your memorizing sessions short—less than an hour. Then you have a manageable collection of facts that can sink into your memory.

Crunch those chunks! Use memory tricks to help bring down the number of chunks of information you need to remember. Suppose you need to memorize the colors that make up the spectrum. That's seven chunks: red, orange, yellow, green, blue, indigo, and violet. Many people use the first letters to make a silly name—ROY G. BIV. This *mnemonic*, or memory helper, breaks seven chunks down to three.

I can do that in my sleep. It's a smart move to memorize or review facts right before bedtime. Your brain doesn't shut down while you sleep—your unconscious mind is actually quite busy, sorting the day's memories. Studying before you turn in actually "programs" your brain to do a little studying even as you sleep. (Keep in mind, though, that this works best when you study a little bit each night over several nights—it doesn't work to wait until the night before a test and then try to force all the facts into your memory right before you fall asleep.)

Essay tests

Studying for single-answer questions is like looking at things through a magnifying glass. Essay questions force you to step back and look at the big picture. Having the facts is helpful, but you have to figure out how to put them together. Here are a few hints.

Unlock those key concepts. You already know how important it is to identify the key concepts and facts. They're the building blocks of any studying system. Go over them; then try to come up with essay questions based on them. The bigger the concept, the more likely it is to turn up as a test question.

Read between the outlines. Once you've come up with a list of possible essay questions, answer them. Come up with outlines to create an essay. Some people go even farther. They write full essays. It's a lot of work, but it is good practice.

Pencil it in. Once you create your study outlines, you still have to remember them. One way to keep all that information in mind is by writing it. If pictures stay in your mind better than words, consider a *mind map*, a memory aid that starts at the center of a page and uses pictures, words, and arrows to make associations between ideas. Here's one to help keep track of facts about the Civil War:

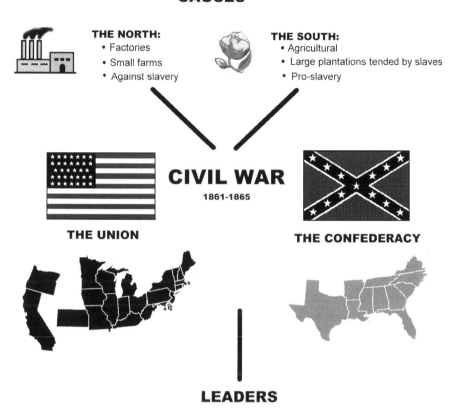

CAUSES

THE NORTH:
- Factories
- Small farms
- Against slavery

THE SOUTH:
- Agricultural
- Large plantations tended by slaves
- Pro-slavery

CIVIL WAR
1861-1865

THE UNION

THE CONFEDERACY

KEY 2

LEADERS

ABRAHAM LINCOLN started the war to preserve the Union. Issuing the Emancipation Proclamation turned the war into a struggle against slavery.

JEFFERSON DAVIS led a very weak government but tried to command the Confederate armies.

U.S. GRANT won victories in the West. Lincoln appointed him to head all the Union armies.

ROBERT E. LEE won battles but lacked troops and supplies to win the war.

Take your time. Taking in the big picture takes longer than memorizing facts in little chunks at a time. Budget big blocks of time—a couple of hours—both to create and review your outline, lists, and mind maps.

Study Groups

You've probably had help from teachers, parents, and friends in the past. But don't forget another source of help in your classroom—the other students around you. Getting together outside of class to study with your fellow students can be a useful tool, often called a *study group.*

Study groups are especially helpful when you choose the members carefully. You don't want to be the smartest person in the group. It might be flattering, but you'll probably get much less help from the other members. You don't want to go the other way, either. If the study group is too high-powered, it may end up leaving you behind. You want a study group that's just right.

Discuss what the test will cover

So far, we've talked about studying what you know, but what about the stuff that you don't know?

Getting someone else's ideas about a test can be an eye-opening experience. You may hear all sorts of things you didn't know. The battle of *what?* The Compromise of *when?* Who is this guy everybody's talking about? What's this short story the class was supposed to read?

Maybe you were out one day, and certain facts weren't in the notes you borrowed. It's a lot better to discover surprises in a study group than stumbling over mystery questions on a test. Besides, information that jumps out at you may surprise someone else in the group. Sharing what you know—and don't know—can help everyone in the group.

Create practice questions

Have everyone in the group come up with a few questions that they think might be on the test. Put all the questions together and practice answering them. If you're lucky, some of these practice questions may actually show up on the test itself.

1. How long does it take you to memorize something? Here are six facts from this chapter, ready to be turned into flash-cards. Copy the questions and answers to the fronts and backs of six index cards. Mix them up; then take fifteen minutes and try to memorize the cards. Put them in a safe place and leave them alone for a week.

FRONT: Research shows that students do best if they study where?
BACK: In the same place

FRONT: What is a good studying snack?
BACK: A piece of fruit

FRONT: Besides chapter headings, where else can you find hints to key concepts in a textbook?
BACK: Subheadings, index pages, and questions at the end of chapters

FRONT: What year did the Civil War end?
BACK: 1865

FRONT: How long should memorizing sessions last?
BACK: No more than one hour

FRONT: If you don't want to write an essay outline, what else can you do?
BACK: Make a mind map

When the week is up, take out the cards. Just looking at the front questions, write down what you think the answers are. When you've done all six, check how close your answers are to the ones on the backs of the cards. How many did you get right? Were your answers close to what was on the card?

Now try using the same cards every day for a week. On the first day, study them for 15 minutes. Every day after them review them for just 5 minutes. At the end of the week, give yourself the same review that you did one week ago: Take out the cards. After just looking at the front questions, write down what you think the answers are. When you've done all six, check how close your answers are to the ones on the backs of the cards. How many did you get right? Were your answers close to what was on the card? In all likelihood, you'll see a great improvement after reviewing the cards every day, compared to letting them sit for a week without review.

You can use this approach with flashcards you make to study for an upcoming test. Get started several weeks ahead of time, and try reviewing every other day. Eventually, you can measure how much study time you need to memorize facts before they really stick in your brain, and how many days can pass before you need to do another review.

2. Set up a study group for one of your most challenging subjects, with six members including yourself. Agree that each person will bring six copies of a practice test that contains: ten short-answer questions, five true/false questions, a ten-item matching column, six multiple-choice questions, and an essay question. That makes 192 practice questions altogether! Of course, there may be some doubles. But there might also be some surprise questions you'd never have thought of.

TAILOR YOUR STUDYING STYLE

✓ **Fill-in-the-Blank Questions**

✓ **True/False Questions**

✓ **Matching Questions**

✓ **Multiple-Choice Questions**

Congratulations on building a good foundation. Now what more can you do to make sure the work you've done fits the test?

K nowing what kinds of questions or statements you'll face on a test is a good starting point, but it's not enough. This part of the book introduces you to the most common test formats, so you'll know how the questions work and how to answer them. The better you understand the types of statements, the better you can do on tests.

Fill-in-the-Blank Questions

Fill-in-the-blank questions have one purpose. They test how well you remember specific facts that you read in your textbook or heard in class. Check out these examples:

The first two battles of the Revolutionary War took place in _ _ _ _ _ _ _ _ _ and _ _ _ _ _ _ _.

Only a _ _ _ _ or a _ _ _ _ _ _ _ can be the subject of a sentence.

The process by which green plants containing chlorophyll use sunlight to turn carbon dioxide and water into sugars, starch, and oxygen is called _ _ _ _ _ _ _ _ _ _ _ _ _ _.

Unless you studied the battles of Lexington and Concord, you couldn't answer Question #1. To answer Question #2, you'd need to know that only a noun or a pronoun can be a subject. And if you didn't know that the exact name for the process in which plants use sunlight to create food is called "photosynthesis," you'd have a tough time trying to answer Question #3.

How do you practice for this kind of statement? First, you have to know the facts. That means your studying must include a good amount of memorization. And make sure you get the spelling right! If the spelling is too far off, the teachers can't tell whether you actually know the word or are taking a wild guess at it.

Sometimes fill-in-the-blank questions come with a list of possible answers off to one side, at the bottom of the page, or on a separate sheet. A list like that can be a big help. It changes your job from recalling a lot of facts to *recognizing* them, which is much easier.

When it comes to fill-in-the-blank tests, the statements themselves can offer a surprising number of clues to help you find the answers.

Read the question carefully

The way a fill-in-the-blank question is written can give you clues. Is there an "a" or "an" in front of the statement's blank? That tells you whether the answer begins with a consonant or a vowel. Do you see "the," "these," or "they?" Those words can tell you whether the correct answer is singular or plural. Yes, they're small clues. But a little jog to your memory might just help you fill in the blank.

Other questions may hide some answers

1. _____ is the capital of Massachusetts.

2. Connecticut is known as the "_____ State."

3. The Green Mountains are found in _____.

4. Cape Cod is found in _____.

You may know the answer to Question #4 is "Massachusetts," but face the problem of not knowing how to spell the state's name! Wait a minute! Massachusetts appears in Question #1, and it's definitely spelled correctly there.

Where have I seen this before?

Often teachers create fill-in-the-blank questions using sentences straight from the textbook. You might be able to "see" the answer by closing your eyes and calling up a picture of the textbook page.

Look closely at the blanks

In the example questions that started this chapter, the blanks actually show how many letters appear in each answer. If that happens on a test, it's a gift! If dashed lines appear on your test, you can ask your teacher if they represent how many letters you should fill in. If blanks are larger or smaller, does that hint how long the answers should be? Does a blank represent one word or several? Every little clue can help jog your memory to fill in those mysterious blanks. Don't hesitate to ask—your teacher may help you with some hints.

True/False Questions

Some students think that true/false questions or statements are there just to be tricky, but that's not the case. True/false questions are designed to test logic and reasoning skills, as well as the ability to read carefully.

As you read your true/false statements, you must pay attention to every word. Just a single word can turn a question into the opposite of what you may think. How should you handle true/false questions?

Read the whole question—carefully

Many students breeze through a question, see something that's true, and figure the whole statement is true. They don't realize that the easiest way to create a false statement is to tack something on that *isn't* true. One little wrong fact can make the whole statement false. For example, a true/false statement may read: "Photosynthesis is the process by which plants and animals use sunlight to create food." If you glance at the phrase and only focus on the words "plants," "sunlight," and "food," you might not notice that the phrase "and animals" was added—even though you clearly know that animals don't use photosynthesis as a food source!

Watch out for super-modifiers

Super-modifers are descriptive words that seem familiar and simple, but because they are general they can create assumptions that aren't completely true—and may even say the exact opposite of what you'd expect. The following super-modifiers can transform what looks like a true sentence into a false one faster than a speeding bullet:

always – never	best – worst
all – none	many – few
more than – less than	absolutely – specifically
neither – both	weak – strong
everybody – nobody	equal to – unequal

The words on the list all go to extremes. For example, consider the sentence, "All Native Americans were hostile to colonists." Just one friendly tribe or person makes that statement untrue. How about this one? "No colonists were rich." If just one colonist who came to America had money, that statement is false.

Watch out for qualifiers

Another type of modifier is a *qualifier*, a word which offers more shades of meaning in a sentence. Because they broaden or expand what a statement is saying, qualifiers in sentences tend to make statements true. Here are some examples:

a majority – a few	often – sometimes
frequently – seldom	probably – unlikely
many – some	usually – rarely
might – may	almost – barely

INSIDE SECRET

Write It Right

Students don't usually worry about their handwriting when they answer true/false questions, but maybe they should. When you're rushing and writing too fast, your "T" could end up looking like an "F" by mistake. If you can, write out "True" or "False" for each statement. If you have room only for one letter, write each answer carefully.

KEY 3

What's the difference? Let's look at two sentences.

1. Luxury cars are always made in America.
2. Many luxury cars are made in America.

Many luxury cars are made in Europe and Japan, so those cars are not *always* built in America. "Always" is a super-modifier that makes

Statement #1 false. However, many luxury cars *are* built in this country. "Many" is a qualifier that makes Statement #2 true.

Beware of negatives

Negatives are words that negate what's being said, so remember to be careful of negatives when they turn up in true/false questions. A statement like "No one who eats fried food is healthy" is false. You can probably think of several people who eat a limited amount of fried food and remain healthy. However, a sentence like "People who eat a large amount of fried food may have higher cholesterol levels" is true.

Things really get tricky when you find *double negatives*—two negative words—in the same sentence. Look at the statement "The Plymouth Colony was not unsuccessful." What is that really saying? The two negative words—"not" and "unsuccessful"—cancel each other out. So the sentence is actually suggesting that "The Plymouth Colony was successful," which is true.

How do you recognize negative words? Many of them begin with the prefixes "un-", "im-", or "mis-"—think of *unclear, impossible, mistake*, and *mislead*. Stay on the lookout for words that start this way, especially if "no" or "not" appear nearby. Remember this advice: It is not unimportant.

Beware of "because"

Another type of sentence to check out carefully is one that uses the word *because*. The word *because* can link two true statements to create a false one! Here's an example.

"Lava comes out of volcanoes because iron melts at 1538 degrees Centigrade."

Both parts of the statement are true. Lava does come out of volcanoes, and the melting point of iron is 1538 degrees Centigrade. However, the melting point of iron doesn't matter because it is *not* the cause of lava flows. The sentence as a whole is false. So, be careful of statements in which the reasons don't match up with the results.

In general, the best way to approach true/false questions is to assume they're true unless you know they are false. Statistically, teachers tend to put more true than false statements in their tests. So if you are totally stumped by a statement, giving a "true" answer means your chances might be a little bit better than fifty-fifty!

Matching Questions

For a matching question or statement test, you get two columns and you have to link an element from one with an item in the other. The match may be a question with an answer, an event with a date, or a word with its synonym. The answers are all there, but they're hiding in a long list. Before you start a test like this, make sure you know the ground rules. For instance, are answers going to be used more than once? Read the instructions carefully.

Doing well on matching column tests doesn't require brain-busting memorization. But you do have to know enough about your subject to make connections and recognize relationships. Begin by carefully reading both lists. Try to see how words on the lists relate to one another. Are they lists of scientists and their discoveries? Explorers and countries? Authors and book titles? This first look primes your brain to start making connections.

If one list is shorter, use that one as your "home base" where you'll note your final choices. Use the second, longer list to give you possibilities to choose from, so you'll have more information to work with.

When trying to make a match, make sure you go through every item on both lists. Sometimes you might see a possible match, but a better one appears farther down the list. Reading every item before you make decisions helps you avoid having to make messy—and time-consuming—changes later.

If words are being used only once, cross off both items when you're sure you've made a match. If you're not sure, make a check to remind yourself that you're leaving the answer "in the mix" in case you find a better match.

After matching all the answers you're sure about, you can start making logical guesses about the remaining matches. Make sure you've made every possible right answer before risking any guesses.

The more matches you make, the better sense you'll get for making connections between columns, so practice this type of question whenever you find a chance— in textbooks, puzzle collections, or even fan magazines.

K
E
Y
3

Multiple-Choice Questions

Ask most students, and they'll probably tell you that multiple-choice tests are their favorites. After all, the answers appear right under the questions or statements. Seems easy, right?

In fact, the best way to start with a multiple-choice question is not to look at the answers at all. See if you can come up with your own answer, which should be fairly easy if you studied for the test. Then check the possibilities and see which comes closest to your answer.

If you face a multiple-choice statement and aren't sure of the answer, you can follow a strategy that uses logic to rule out certain answers and narrow down the possible answers. Since multiple-choice questions usually have four possible answers, you have a one in four chance of getting the right answer if you simply rely on guessing. One right answer out of four means you've got a 25 percent possibility of getting the right answer—or a 75 percent chance of getting the wrong one.

You can improve on that percentage if you use the process of elimination to rule out any answers you know are wrong. If you can knock out one wrong answer, your chances of success go up to 33 percent. If you knock out two wrong answers, your chances go up to 50 percent. Knock out three, and—hey! You've got the right answer!

The following tips show ways that you can weed out wrong answers and look for better possibilities:

Longer answers usually deserve a closer look. A teacher often adds special details to make sure that students recognize the correct answer, so paying attention to long choices may help you.

When the answers involve numbers, you may be able to eliminate some of the choices without knowing the exact answer. Check out this example:

The height of the Washington Monument is

A. 25 feet.
B. 100 feet.
C. 555 feet.
D. 1,200 feet.

Well, you probably know that 25 feet is too small. And 1,200 feet would put the monument in the same league as some of the world's tallest skyscrapers. The two middle choices seem more realistic. If you studied, no doubt the 555 figure would jump out at you. See if you can knock out the extreme answers to these kinds of questions. Usually, the correct answer is found in the middle range.

Be on guard when two answers seem almost alike. It's likely that one of them is the correct answer for the statement—and the other one is a confusing "double." Often these types of answers are especially long, so take that as another clue that you should be paying extra attention. Take this statement, for example:

In Native American culture, *wampum* was

A. a war-cry.
B. strings of polished wood beads used for decorating canoes.
C. strings of polished shells used both as money and jewelry.
D. a breakfast food.

Answer B is very similar to C. A careless reader might jump on the words "string" and "polished" in B—and choose the wrong answer. Answer C has the correct description, "strings of polished shells" and also the correct use, "money and jewelry."

Use grammar as a clue. A grammar check of a multiple-choice question might help you find the answer. Take a look at this question:

The major reason the Pilgrims came to America was

A. Pilgrims were Separatists.
B. to practice their religion freely.
C. dislike of Holland and fear of war.
D. fur trading.

The correct answer is B. Answer A is a separate sentence that does not fit grammatically with the start of the question. Answer C gives two reasons while the question asks for one reason—singular. Grammar clues alone eliminate two of the four answers.

Trust your ability to recognize familiar details. As you work through the answers, stay on the lookout for names, dates, and facts that got a lot of attention in your textbook or in class. Because those types of information are items you should have studied, teachers often add those important details to help you point out correct answers. On the other hand, be suspicious of answers with unfamiliar information—they're likely to be made up.

KEY
3

Apply tips for answering true/false statements to tackling the multiple-choice challenge. After all, you're looking for a true statement—it's just hiding among three false ones. Negative words, super modifiers, and qualifiers can play important parts in helping you choose the correct answers.

Always pay close attention to the instructions. Read instructions on the test paper carefully, and pay attention to what your teacher says. You may discover, for instance, that there's more than one correct answer per question. Or you may find something like, "All of the following answers are true *except* one."

Filling in Bubble Forms

Most multiple-choice tests are pretty simple. Either you mark your answers right on the test paper or you write them on a separate sheet of notebook paper. Nowadays, more and more schools are giving standardized tests with special answer sheets called *bubble forms*.

Reading	Science	Social Studies
1 Ⓐ Ⓑ Ⓒ Ⓓ	1 Ⓐ Ⓑ Ⓒ Ⓓ	1 Ⓐ Ⓑ Ⓒ Ⓓ
2 Ⓐ Ⓑ Ⓒ Ⓓ	2 Ⓐ Ⓑ Ⓒ Ⓓ	2 Ⓐ Ⓑ Ⓒ Ⓓ
3 Ⓐ Ⓑ Ⓒ Ⓓ	3 Ⓐ Ⓑ Ⓒ Ⓓ	3 Ⓐ Ⓑ Ⓒ Ⓓ

These bubble form answer sheets look simple enough. Usually, they're just row after row of blank rectangles or circles—which is why they're called "bubbles"—where you use a pencil to fill in the answer next to the number of each question. Hundreds, even thousands, of test answers can be graded quickly using a computer. This is an efficient way to assess your learning almost instantly. However, this system has a downside—it doesn't forgive even the smallest error.

Let's say you're taking a 100-question test. By mistake, you skip over a line, filling in the answer for Question #48 in the space meant for Question #49. When it comes to grading, the computer simply marks every answer from that point on as wrong.

Also, be aware that some test answers are arranged left to right in rows, while others fall in columns down the page. Make sure that you follow the correct order when writing your answer, and be careful that you don't skip an answer by mistake.

Follow these tips for keeping forms from bursting your bubble:

Pay attention to the instructions. Carefully read the directions for the test, especially the instructions on the cover of the test booklet. They may have differences from the tests you've practiced. If the teacher in charge of the test gives spoken instructions, make sure you listen carefully. If you don't understand an instruction, ask the person in charge to explain it again.

Keep track of your place. Fold your test booklet so only one page of questions shows. This helps you keep track of which question you're working on. You can't fold your answer page, but you can do something similar to make sure the right answers go on the right lines. If you're allowed to use scrap paper, line up one blank sheet under the first line of bubbles. After you've answered Question #1, move the sheet to reveal the bubbles for Question #2, and so on. If you're not allowed to bring scrap paper, use your extra pencil as your line marker.

Match, match, match. Every four or five questions, check that the number of the question matches the number on the answer line. This can save you a lot of backtracking time (and grief!) if the numbers don't match. Also, whenever you have to turn a page in the test booklet, make sure the top statement number matches the number of the line where you need to put your next answer. This helps you avoid the possibility that two pages might get stuck together.

Neatness counts. Computers can't tell one pencil mark from another, so don't leave stray marks on the answer sheet. If you have to change an answer, make sure the old one is erased completely.

Working with bubble forms can take a little getting used to. When you become comfortable with the bubble forms, the standardized tests become a matter of what you know, not how the test is formatted.

KEY 3

Ready, Set, *REVIEW*

1. To practice working with true/false questions, write ten statements for someone else to answer. First, choose a friend or family member who might be willing to take a test. Then pick a topic that you both know about. For example, if your best friend is on your soccer team, make soccer your topic. Next, come up with ten *true* statements about soccer. Now, select five and change them by adding one or two words that make them false. If you're really careful about which words you choose, you can trick your friend into picking a wrong answer. Give it a try!

2. Practicing test questions doesn't have to revolve around assigned homework. When it comes to matching questions, your friends, parents, and other family members can come up with lists for you to match. Of course they can create the list from material they find in your textbook and study notes. But you also can practice matching information on subjects outside of school. Do you like to read? Maybe someone can make up a list of characters and books. Are sports your thing? Maybe you can match the members of your favorite team with their positions. Or maybe you can link sports teams to their hometowns. For music fans, you might match musicians to their bands, singers to the style of music they make, or lines of songs to titles. These exercises can help you feel comfortable using test-taking skills, and show you that tests can even be fun.

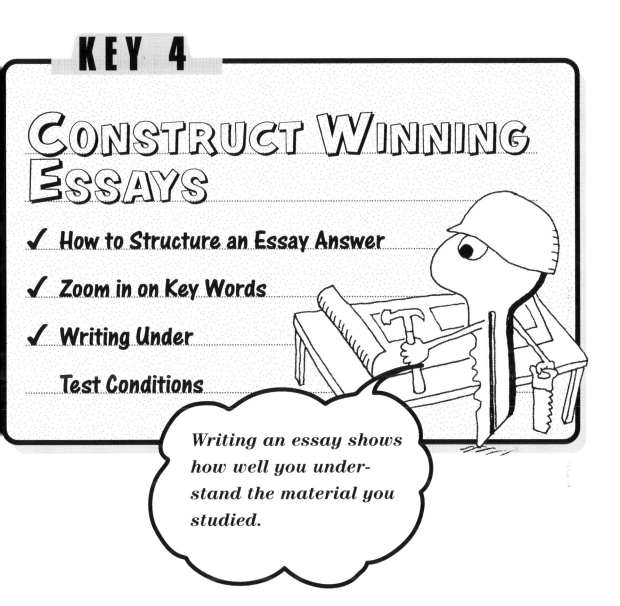

CONSTRUCT WINNING ESSAYS

✓ **How to Structure an Essay Answer**

✓ **Zoom in on Key Words**

✓ **Writing Under**

Test Conditions

Writing an essay shows how well you understand the material you studied.

O f all the test questions students must face, essays probably get rated as the toughest. That's because you don't just come up with an answer and move on.

How can you practice for essay questions? One way is pre-test awareness. When you study, pay special attention to topics that were discussed a lot in class. These important points often turn up as essay questions. What definitions and lists went up on the blackboard? These probably play an important part in essays. What is emphasized in any handouts or study guides the teacher gave you? What points are stressed in any pre-test reviews?

You also should practice setting up outlines. Any class you take has only a limited number of major topics. While you study, work up outlines for at least the top ten topics. You might be surprised to find that your test paper has a question exactly like one that you've outlined. Then you'll already have a logical framework for constructing your essay.

Finally, you can practice essays by writing them. With essay questions, you need to organize and support what you know. So you must be familiar with the parts of an essay and how to put them together.

How to Structure an Essay Answer

The first step in constructing an essay for a test is to budget your time. Watch the clock as you practice, so you can set up a realistic schedule to cover the main ideas.

Next, read the essay question carefully. Find the key words that give directions, like "describe," "compare," or "convince." Circle them. Those words set out the writing job you have to do. Make sure you understand the question.

Once you understand the question, write a brief outline. The outline should take the form of a list of points you want to cover. After jotting down your ideas, take a little time to number them in a logical order.

Next, you need to work on the *introductory statement*. This is the sentence that shows the teacher that you understand what the question is asking. It also sets up how you intend to answer it. A simple way to create your introductory statement is to change the test question into the beginning of your statement, followed by words that show where you plan to go with your essay. Follow up the introductory statement by introducing the key points that make up your answer. Each of these key points will become the main topic of each new paragraph that follows.

With each new paragraph, bring in the next key point to create a *topic sentence*. Develop this main topic of each paragraph by presenting facts, examples, and details that support it. Use language that connects your ideas, such as: "There are three states of matter . . ."; "By the 1700s, the French controlled a larger part of North America, but the British colonies had a much larger population . . ."; or "Although wooden furniture does not seem like a living thing, it actually is organic. . . ."

In your last paragraph, you need to summarize by restating the concept you started off with in a way that ties everything together. This should be easy to do since this is what you've been building toward in the middle paragraphs.

Zoom in on Key Words

All words in a sentence are not equal. This is certainly true with test questions—especially essay questions. If the question asks you to compare two books and you only describe one of them, you are not fully answering the question.

Key words offer valuable instructions. If you're allowed to write on your test paper, circle the key words in every essay question. Doing that can help you keep your mind on your task and focus on exactly what you're supposed to do. The following section shows how each key word sets out your job for you.

Show you know the facts

Essay questions have one thing in common with the shorter types of exam questions. You still have to know the facts. To write an essay, however, you have to show that you can put the facts to use. The most basic job you can do with facts is to put them together to make a coherent presentation or convincing argument. Here's how you can do that in response to each of the following key words.

Summarize

To summarize, your essay should cover the main points about a subject, without a lot of unnecessary details. For a successful essay of this kind, you have to know the facts, and then pick out the important ones. You have to be brief and to the point, reducing a large subject to the bare details.

Describe

In a descriptive essay, your job is to draw—in words—a picture of a person, place, thing, or idea. You want to use details to identify all the main parts involved. For example, if you're describing a process, go through it step by step. Show that you know the facts by making your picture as complete as possible.

Show you understand

Many essay questions ask for more than summaries or descriptions of the facts. They want you to demonstrate that you are able to understand what the facts mean, see relationships, and explain where things are going.

Analyze

Analyzing a subject is like taking a machine apart to see how it works. Your essay has to break down whatever you're writing about into pieces, factors, or relationships. Then you have to show how the whole thing comes together to work. Your attention must focus on the way the elements you describe relate to one another. Often, you're using the information to reach some sort of conclusion or personal judgment.

Compare

When an essay question asks you to compare persons, events, things, or ideas, you should first look for similarities the two items share. After you've shown they are alike, examine their differences. Essentially, the job comes down to working up a pair of descriptions and finding relationships between the qualities or characteristics you've outlined.

Contrast

Finding a contrast between items is the flip side of comparing them. Where a comparison emphasizes similarities, a contrast focuses on differences. To begin, you must examine the two people, events, or ideas you've been asked to contrast. List the basic facts about them, pair up the characteristics, and evaluate them. Then find the ways in which they're different. Once you've done that, you're ready to begin writing your essay.

Classify

Classifying essays are not commonly given. When they are, you are given a number of items to group together and then give a name to each group. When you classify, part of the job is like comparing the items—you're looking for similarities. You also need to know about the categories you'll be sorting them into. Half the battle is figuring out how the various items relate to one another. Then you have to compare them, put them in the proper classes, and explain your decision.

Predict

When an essay question asks you to predict, it usually provides a situation with various kinds of information. Based on what you know, you

K
E
Y

4

have to decide on a solution or result and explain your decision. This is perhaps the most open-ended type of essay question. Often, most of the information you'll work with comes with the question, rather than from facts you've studied.

While the facts may all be in the question, you must make your prediction based on the ideas you've studied. Your understanding of a particular short story must come from the other short stories you've read. Figuring out the results of a science experiment depends on how much science you understand from your course studies.

Show you can evaluate

You've seen essays that present information and essays that explore relationships between facts. With other essay questions, however, you have to look at facts and decide how to use them—usually to present a case. Sometimes the job involves balancing facts to come to a judgment or a decision. For many of these essay questions, you're writing to persuade the reader, so you must decide which are the most convincing facts to include in your essay.

Judge

When you're asked to judge something, you face a four-part job. First, you analyze the subject, breaking it down into its elements. Next, you must compare and then contrast these items, looking at different facts, good and bad, for or against the idea you're discussing. Then, you have to present your case, before, finally, coming to a conclusion. This is trickier than simply listing facts or finding relationships. You have to go over the facts and see what convinces you. Often, a subject has many sides. You have to present them all, consider the evidence, and then wrap it up.

The important part of judging a subject is weighing the evidence, the advantages and limitations of each argument, to come to a conclusion. With all essays where you have to evaluate and comment, take care to distinguish which parts of the essay offer facts as evidence and which parts offer your opinion.

Decide

When an essay question asks you to decide about a subject, the job is much like judging. Instead of balancing the pros and cons, however, you select among several choices and defend your decision. While deciding means evaluating various choices, it's not about choosing at random. You have to work from the facts you've studied, so you have to know them fairly well. Organize your facts as evidence to back up the choice you made.

Support

When you're asked to write a "support" essay, the question may set out a particular position or ask you to pick one. Either way, you must form facts into a framework that bolsters a specific position. You must review what you know about the subject, and come up with the best case possible.

Evaluating information for a "support" essay doesn't involve balancing viewpoints or judgments. Your point of view is already set. You don't have to present the other side. All you have to do is build up a solid case based on facts from your textbook or from class discussions. If you're giving your own opinion, make sure to distinguish that from factual evidence.

Convince

What is the difference between writing an essay to support an idea and an essay to convince someone to think about an idea in a certain way? When you come down to it, both take a position on a topic and try to come up with a strong case for it. The difference is that the word "convince" shows that the aim of this kind of essay is to persuade a reader.

GETTING IT RIGHT

Key Words for Writing Essays

Here's a chart to help you remember the different kinds of essay direction words.

Key Word	What You Should Do	Sample Essay Questions
Summarize	Reduce a subject to its main points.	Summarize the events of the Constitutional Convention.
Describe	Present a picture in words.	Describe how an internal combustion engine works.
Analyze	Break a subject into its elements and discuss their relationships.	Analyze the Union strategy during the Civil War.
Compare	Find the similarities between two items.	Compare the character of Tom Sawyer with that of Huckleberry Finn.
Contrast	Find the differences between two items.	Contrast the novels *Tom Sawyer* and *Huckleberry Finn*.
Classify	Break items down into groups.	Classify the original thirteen American colonies by type.
Predict	Examine facts to come up with a result.	Having read Frank R. Stockton's "The Lady, Or the Tiger?," predict the ending.
Judge	Examine the good and bad points about a subject.	Judge whether the Constitution's system of checks and balances still works today.
Decide	Use facts to come to a conclusion.	Decide which was the major factor in the Confederacy losing the Civil War.
Support	Organize facts to back up a given idea.	Support the theory that a giant meteor strike caused the extinction of the dinosaurs.
Convince	Present facts to prove something is true.	Convince the reader that the Bill of Rights was a necessary addition to the Constitution.
Argue	Give a strong case for a position using evidence and disproving opposing viewpoints.	Argue whether or not uniforms should be worn at public schools.

You use evidence and logic to get someone to agree with you. Usually, these subjects turn out to be more controversial than factual.

Argue

When you're asked to argue in an essay, you progress beyond merely trying to convince the reader. You still use evidence and logic to make your case, but you also have to acknowledge what the other side might say—then show that your points are superior. In other words, you have to act as though you were in an actual argument or debate.

Just as when you write to convince people, the more controversial the topic, the better. Often, beginning with a question as you argue can be helpful. Answering that question becomes your introductory statement. You just need to stick to the point as you develop your argument. Not only do you have to give lots of facts and evidence for your side, but you have to present the opposing side—and demolish its case. As with all persuasive writing, you have to let the reader know what is fact and what is opinion.

Writing Under Test Conditions

You've identified the key words for writing essays and understand how they help you approach the different types you might be called to write. Now you need to get down to the nitty-gritty: How do you write one of these essays during a test, when you're under time pressure? Here are strategies for handling the job.

Taking notes during tests

You've already read about taking notes in class, but you might want to try taking take notes during tests! If some key facts or ideas pop into your head just as you read a test question, jot them down while they're fresh in your memory. Remember that test notes don't have to be a work of art—the most important thing is that you can read them.

KEY 4

When it comes time to write your essay, the first step is making notes. Whether you're showing, understanding, or evaluating, take a few moments to write the main facts and points you know about the topic in the question. For the moment, you're *brainstorming*—trying to come up with as many ideas as possible. After you have the facts on your scrap paper, start going over them with a critical eye. Which are the most important? Which are less important? You'll probably end up crossing out a number of items. To keep your essay concise, trim your information until everything is essential. Then you can start organizing it.

Outline

Your outline forms the framework for constructing your essay. It's the blueprint that helps you organize your facts and ideas, so it must reflect what's included in your basic essay. For example, many essays contain five paragraphs: an introductory paragraph, explaining the purpose of the essay and presenting the introductory statement; three body paragraphs that present facts, evidence, or examples; and a concluding paragraph that sums up all this material.

Look over your rough list of ideas. Choose the three strongest to form your body paragraphs. Number these ideas in the order you think they should appear. Look at the rest of your list. If there are more points that must be made, decide whether to number them to create additional paragraphs, or whether to use them as supporting facts for existing paragraphs.

For supporting facts, just draw an arrow from the fact to the numbered paragraph topic where it belongs. If you have time, make a new list with all your paragraph topics and their supporting facts in order. If you have more than five main ideas, look carefully to decide whether they are all necessary. If you could get by without some of them, cross them out.

Drafting

Once you've got your ideas in order, it's time to start the actual writing. If you have lots of time, you might consider doing a rough draft of the whole answer. Unfortunately, most tests don't allow that much time.

Try to at least work up a draft of your first paragraph. If you can mark your test paper, circle the key words in the essay question. Now you can start coming up with your introductory statement, which sets up what you're about to present and may even hint at your conclusion.

KEY 4

If you had to answer the essay question, "Describe the Battle of Gettysburg," which is the better beginning?

The Battle of Gettysburg was fought on July 1, 2, and 3, 1863.

Or:

A crucial battle of the Civil War, the Battle of Gettysburg marked the last Confederate attempt to invade Union states.

The first example gives facts, but the second example actually begins to describe the battle.

Once you've set up your introductory statement, use the rest of the first paragraph to set up the three main points you're going to use. For the Gettysburg essay we just started, those facts might be:

The opposing armies didn't have a plan—they just bumped into each other.

The battle took place over three days.

Robert E. Lee gambled on a final assault—Pickett's Charge—that failed horribly.

Think of other facts to insert as you write the body of the essay. Dates, places, commanders, and events in the battle can all help to back up these major topics and fill in the paragraphs. Probably the best way to organize this answer is chronologically—step by step as the battle unfolded.

The final paragraph of the essay also demands special care, so a practice draft will help if you have time. In four or so sentences, this paragraph should sum up everything in the essay and relate it all to the introductory statement. Going back to the Gettysburg example:

At the end of the battle the Confederates were forced to retreat, but the Union army was too exhausted to pursue them. While neither army entered the battle with a plan and both armies were exhausted after three long days of fighting, the failure of General Lee's risky assault was a turning point in the war. After Gettysburg, Lee's army was never strong enough to go on the attack again.

As you write your essay, remember to keep tying things together. To show how events followed one another, use connecting phrases like, "First," "second," and "third," or "At the beginning," "next," and "and then." This helps to guide the reader through your work.

Revision

Essays may be written quickly, but they're graded at a slower pace. Things you missed in your hurry to write are spotted by a more leisurely reader—mistakes like misspellings, words you meant to put in but didn't, and phrases that don't quite make sense. A good rule of thumb is to allow about 10 percent of your writing time to check over what you did.

If you have the space on your answer paper to do it, try skipping lines as you write your essay. That way, during your revision you can cross out mistakes and write them in neatly or even insert whole sentences. Look for yourself, and decide which is easier to read:

INSIDE SECRET

Answer only part of the question

What should you do if a test has an essay question that you *almost* know the answer to? First, answer any questions you do know. Then, just start organizing the one you're less sure about. Work up the parts you understand, and then tackle the mystery section. Do your best on the weak spot and concentrate on the other parts of the answer— that way you can get partial credit.

KEY 4

GETTING IT RIGHT

Neatness counts, even if you might think it doesn't. You want the person marking your test to feel as good as possible about your paper. That's less likely to happen if the person is constantly squinting in an effort to decipher sloppy handwriting and a messy essay.

Gen Cornwallis ~~thinks~~ thought Yorktown WAS a ~~good~~ safe place to bring his army. The town was a port on chesapeake Bay. Brit. ships could bring in ~~things~~ supplies. But a French fleet ~~was~~ appeared, blocking ~~off~~ the British. French also landed UNDER General Rochambeau. They joined forces with Washington, who had led his troops south. The B ARMY was trapped by land and by sea.

General Cornwallis thought Yorktown was a safe place to bring

his army. The town was a port on Chesapeake Bay. British ships

could bring in supplies. But a French fleet appeared, blocking off

the British. French soldiers also landed under General Rochambeau.

They joined forces with George Washington, who had led his

troops south. The British army was trapped by land and by sea.

K
E
Y
4

1. Outlines are the framework for any essay. Create an outline to frame an answer to this question:

   "If you do well on essay questions, describe the steps you take during a test to write a successful essay. If you do not do well on essays, describe suggestions that might help you improve."

2. Now write an essay that answers the question in #1 (above). Try timing yourself while you work—give yourself 25 minutes to write. Don't forget to allow yourself time to review!

MASTER YOUR TEST-TAKING STRATEGIES

✓ **Open-Book Test Secrets**

✓ **Understand the Instructions**

✓ **If You're Stuck**

✓ **Time Management**

Study time is finally over? What do you do now?

First of all, stay calm. This is the day you've been preparing for. You've been studying the right way, so you won't face any surprises that may come in the test material.

Next, remind yourself that you can feel confident about your test-taking skills. After going through the tips in this section, you'll have gained insight into important strategies to follow when taking any test.

Don't forget to bring everything you need for the test. You've scheduled your study hours, and you've scheduled your review sessions. This isn't the day to lose track of time. You don't want to run around like a maniac, forgetting stuff. Aim to get to the classroom a little early, and be ready when you arrive. It helps to have your supplies ready the night before. What does this include?

- 2 pencils

- 2 pens with similar-colored ink

- An eraser

- Lots of scrap paper (if it's allowed)

- A calculator (if you need to do math)

- A spare battery for the calculator

- A watch to keep careful track of time during the test

- Your textbook and notes, if this is an open-book test.

Open-Book Test Secrets

Many students think that open-book tests are really easy. You can get the answers right out of your book and notes. Why do you even have to study?

You can't expect to answer questions on this type of test by simply copying a list of facts from your book. The reason you're allowed to refer to your books is so that you won't spend your study time memorizing. Instead, you'll have to analyze and organize facts from tables and listings and discuss important concepts by putting together topics from their texts. That means finding those topics and putting them together—usually in essay questions.

As for not having to study, think again. To do well on an open-book test, you have to know the same sort of concepts and key topics needed to answer essay questions. And you have to know where they are in your book and notes so you can refer to them!

Students who don't prepare for open-book tests often spend too much time flipping through pages, frantically searching for a particular heading or section, instead of answering questions. Prepared students know where key topics are.

Since schools usually own your textbooks, you usually aren't allowed to write in them. But you can use paper clips to mark important pages. Even better, use bookmarks or sticky notes to set off important topics. You can even write the topics on your place markers to help you find them quickly. In your own notebook, you can underline, use highlighter, paper clips, bookmarks, or even tabs to speed up your search.

Don't overdo it by marking every little item. The idea is to make important topics stand out, not to get them lost in a crowd. To help find less important headings, single facts, and other smaller bits of information, use your study list of important topics that you keep in your notes. If you mark the page numbers from the textbook beside the headings on your list, you'll have a do-it-yourself index of all the important points for class. That can be helpful when you're reviewing for a test later, and it can be a lifesaver during an open-book test.

KEY 5

Understand the Instructions

Now you're ready to tackle that test. Don't forget to take the time to check the instructions. You might know everything necessary to answer the questions, but you can miss crucial points if you don't understand the rules. Are you supposed to write on the test sheet itself, or do your answers go on a separate piece of paper or into a special booklet? The moments before the test are often when you find out things like this, so listen and read carefully.

The most ordinary instructions can confuse you if you're not careful. Suppose you only have to answer one essay question out of three. If you don't read that instruction, you might work on all three essays. Think of the time you'd waste! You might be putting a lot of effort into writing three rushed essays instead of investing the time in one well-written one.

To show the importance of instructions, some teachers have given out test papers where the top paragraph says, "Answer every fifth question." You'd be surprised at how many students answered the whole test. That will never happen to you, though, now that you've learned to read before you write.

Spoken instructions

Here comes your teacher with the test sheets. Before the papers get passed out, the teacher has a few words to say. Pay close attention. These last-minute instructions may change the information printed on the test paper. Whatever your teacher has to tell you in these moments is golden. Pay attention and you may discover helpful suggestions to improve your performance.

Written instructions

Now the test is in your hands. The first thing to do is read the printed instructions. You might discover all kinds of crucial information. How many questions are you supposed to answer? What kinds of answers are you supposed to give? These and other questions can be resolved if you read the top of the sheet or the first page of the test booklet. Some teachers often list how many points each section of the test is worth. That helps you decide how much time you should spend on each group of questions.

GETTING IT RIGHT

Examples of unusual instructions

You've taken lots of tests already. So you might ask, "How unusual can instructions get?" Check out these unusual instructions, and then identify the main words that give you clues to cracking their unusual code. Following the examples, you can find an explanation to help you discover if you cracked the code correctly:

SAMPLE TEST INSTRUCTIONS

A. Organize the following events in chronological order, from the most to the least recent.

B. The Louisiana Purchase took place between which of the following events? All of the following are true except …

C. Over which of the following countries has the British flag never flown?

D. Please cross off every correct answer.

EXPLANATIONS

A. When people see the word "chronological," they usually start in the past and work up to the present, not the other way around.

B. This is a challenging multiple-choice instruction because *except* isn't in large or italic type.

C. Beware of the negative word that turns an instruction topsy-turvy.

D. This is a multiple-choice challenge because you'd expect to cross out incorrect answers.

KEY 5

If You're Stuck

It can happen sometimes. You studied hard. You knew it last
night . . . but at test time, you stare at a question and the answer
won't come. What do you do?

Go over the question again, carefully. Do you understand what it
says? Can you put the question in your own words? What's the basic
concept in the question? Are there any clues inside the question itself?
Can you remember your teacher talking about it? Was there any class
discussion about this particular idea? Can you visualize the textbook
page from your memory to "see" the concept?

If you still can't come up with an answer, put a check by the question and move on. The worst thing you can do is fall into "test-day
daze," stalling out at the one question that baffles you when you *can*
answer lots of others. You can't afford to waste precious minutes, so
move on. You may get a clue later on in the test or the answer may pop
up in your memory. At least you're doing something positive—answering other important questions.

When to guess and when to leave it blank

On some exams, you get points solely for how many questions you get
right. Incorrect answers don't count. Other times, you may receive two
points for being correct, but lose a point for incorrect answers. For
other tests, incorrect answers may lose you the full number of points—
and so does leaving an answer blank.

Most tests explain these ground rules in the directions. If not, ask
your teacher. Once you know the rules, you can make a decision. Why
not guess, then, if there's no penalty, you have a 25 percent chance of
"winning."

If you lose as many points for leaving a blank as you get for a
wrong answer, you probably should take a guess. Suppose you've got a

multiple-choice question and you've ruled out two of the four answers. Is it worth the fifty-fifty risk? If you've figured that two answers on a multiple-choice question seem true and one of the remaining answers is "all of the above," it might be worth the risk to choose that one.

Smart guessing strategies

When people talk about "guessing strategies," they don't mean closing your eyes and plunking a finger down. You could refer to this process as "critical thinking and subconscious selection," but "guessing" is much shorter.

There are two basic rules about guessing. First, never make wild guesses. Always have a reason for your choice. Second, your first guess is usually your best guess. Don't change an answer unless you have a good reason—like getting a clue from another question. Noticing that the last four questions were "B" on a multiple-choice test is *not* a good reason to change an answer.

If something "looks" wrong on a true/false or a multiple-choice question, trust your gut instinct. After putting a lot of effort into studying, you may discover that you know more than you consciously realize.

KEY 5

Using categories as guessing clues

When matching columns and a variety of items, look for categories of information. Suppose you come up with answers for all but three questions—a name, a date, and a place. If the two columns have equal numbers of items, you should be able to find your answers fairly easily by deciding which category they fit in. For example, a statement that says an event occurred "on" is likely to match up with a date, while a statement that says an event happened "at" or "in" is likely to match up with the name of a place.

Categories of answers may help you respond to multiple-choice questions, too. Look for opposites because they suggest that one of the two is correct, as in this question:

The Tropic of Capricorn is in

A. the Northern Hemisphere.

B. Europe.

C. Australia.

D. the Southern Hemisphere.

The answer is D. The Tropic of Capricorn is an imaginary line that circles the Earth in the Southern Hemisphere.

Another category to look for is the answer that is most inclusive, or broad. This principle also worked in the previous question because hemispheres cover more area than continents.

True/false strategies also apply when choosing answers that focus on categories of information. Here's a possible multiple-choice question about history:

The colony of New Amsterdam allowed

A. only Dutch settlers.

B. some English settlers.

C. settlers from many lands.

D. only Protestants.

The correct answer is C—besides the Dutch, there were French Protestants and Jewish people from Portugal in New Amsterdam. Two of the answers began with "only" an extreme super-modifier that restricts the answers. The other two choices used qualitative words— "some" and "many" to offer a wider range of possibilities. If it comes down to making a tough choice, be wary of the extreme responses and look carefully at the more inclusive possibilities.

Sometimes, though, you may have to narrow your search between several true statements to find the right answer. Your job then is to choose the most complete response. Take a look at this question:

A square has
A. four sides.
B. three sides and a tail.
C. four equal sides.
D. the same number of sides as a polygon.

Answers B and D are just plain wrong. But answers A and C are both true. A square does have four sides, but so does a rectangle. The most complete answer is that a square has four equal sides, so C is the most correct answer.

A special category among multiple-choice questions is the joke or the completely unfamiliar answer. Think for a moment about the teacher's job when creating a test. To include 25 multiple-choice questions, the teacher has to come up with 75 wrong answers. It should come as no surprise that a teacher might use an entirely unknown term or put in a joke just for fun or to help students lighten up. If you studied, choices using unfamiliar phrases can be safely rejected. If you come across a funny response, enjoy the joke and silently thank your teacher for helping you to eliminate one answer.

You've practiced answering various test questions on material you've studied. Is it possible to train yourself at guessing too? As you work on practice tests, use a check to mark the questions where you guessed. As you go over the answers, pay attention to those check-marks. You may discover concepts you do not understand or areas that

KEY 5

you should be studying. Also, you can get a sense of how successful your guessing strategy would be on a real test.

Time Management

Remember the beginning of this chapter, where you were supposed to bring everything you need to the test? Among those items was a watch. From the moment you start looking at the test paper, ask questions like, "How much time should I spend on these matching columns?" and "How much time will I need to answer these multiple-choice questions?"

Sometimes each section of an examination is timed—you can't move ahead or back once that time is up. This often happens with standardized tests. In those cases, you have to make the best of the time you have for each part of the test.

On tests where you can decide how much time to spend on each section, budget your time and then stick to your schedule. As you look over the test paper, two questions should stand out in you mind: "How easily can I do each section?" and "How many points is each section worth?"

Set your own pace and stick to it. Pay no attention to the other students. If they scribble frantically or take it easy, that may be what works best for them. You've studied and done enough practice questions to know your own speed. Do the best *you* can.

Don't spend too much time on one question

You recognize the dangers of "test-day daze." If the answer doesn't come quickly, skip the question and go on to ones you can answer. You can come back after you've finished the other questions, when you might have found a clue somewhere on the test. Sometimes, your brain keeps working on a question behind the scenes, and the answer pops into your head five or ten questions farther along.

Taylor had a bad case of the Test-Day Daze.

Do the fastest, easiest part first

Some people like to tackle the hardest question in a test first. However, this approach has a risk. You might get bogged down and lose time that could have been spent getting more points on simpler questions.

Are you a multiple-choice champ? A matching-question whiz? Starting out with questions you know you can handle easily helps build your confidence. This approach is especially helpful when the questions also are worth a lot of points.

As you work through the test, keep choosing sections based on how easy they are for you and how many points they're worth. Often this approach leaves essay questions for last, which is where budgeting every minute really becomes important. You need to divide your remaining time between outlining your ideas and writing up your answers—and remember to allow time for a review.

Check your answers

It happens on every test. Halfway through the time (or so it seems), somebody gets up and hands in his or her paper. There's usually a gasp or a moan from everybody else, and they start writing more frantically.

Relax. This is a test, not a race with the person who sits next to you. People don't get extra points for finishing early. As you set up your schedule for a test, leave time for reviewing at the end. Experts suggest using as much as 10 percent of your time for this job. This means that if you have forty-five minutes to take the test, you should save four to five minutes at the end to review your answers.

You have a lot to do. Have you answered all the questions you're supposed to answer? Is everything you wrote legible? How is your grammar and spelling? If you transferred answers from scrap paper, did you copy correctly? How are your essays? Were you in such a hurry to get things written down that you may have skipped a word here or there? A final check makes sure that you got everything down on paper to the best of your ability.

INSIDE SECRET

1. You've seen some examples of confusing instructions in this chapter. Does your teacher sometimes give trick questions? Check through old tests and homework assignments, and find the five most unusual instructions your teacher has given. Share these examples with your study group. Your classmates may come up with other examples of instructions to look out for.

2. Get some extra practice taking a timed test by reading the following questions. Then answer only questions 1, 2, 4, and 6. The other questions are distractions. If you have a timer, set it for ten minutes. If not, time ten minutes on a clock.

   1. It is not unadvisable to check the entire test for instructions when you get the paper. T F

   2. One of the best strategies for answering a multiple-choice question is to treat it like
   A. a box full of rattlesnakes.
   B. a matching question with four columns.
   C. a true/false question.
   D. all of the above.

   3. You are taking a test that runs for two hours (120 minutes). There are 10 multiple-choice questions worth 30 out of 100 points. How much time should you spend checking the answers in this section?
   A. thirty minutes
   B. ten minutes
   C. 1.2 minutes
   D. ten seconds

K
E
Y

5

4. Match the following question types with guessing strategies for answering them:

A. Matching questions   1) the most complete answer

B. Multiple-choice questions   2) something "looks" wrong

C. True/false questions   3) spotting categories of answers

5. It is best to guess the answer to a question
   A. when you can't cheat from your neighbor's paper.
   B. when you're too tired to think.
   C. when you're running out of time.
   D. all of the above.

6. Teachers make many questions using sentences directly from the textbook. T F

7. Write a four-paragraph essay describing the best time-budgeting strategies for taking a test.

ANSWERS: 1: T; 2: C; 4: A-3, B-1, C-2; 6: T (You *did* notice the note about answering only Questions 1, 2, 4 and 6, didn't you?)

TAKE CONTROL OF TEST ANXIETY

✓ **What Is Test Anxiety?**

✓ **Facing Test Anxiety**

✓ **Ways to Relax**

> *Remember to take a deep breath. Remind yourself that everything is going to be fine.*

You've worked hard, and test day has come. As you walk into school, somebody comes up to you. "What's the capital of Armenia?" they ask, looking panicked.

Wait a minute—wasn't this supposed to be an English test? You realize the student is from another class, but you still feel an anxious quiver in your stomach. By the time you sit down for the exam, your palms are sweating. Your stomach is gurgling—maybe it was a bad idea to have donuts and soda for breakfast. . . .

When the test paper arrives, you're afraid to look at it, for fear nothing will seem familiar. The top of the answer sheet says "Name." That's familiar enough!

What Is Test Anxiety?

That opening story describes a few of the symptoms that some people feel when they think about taking a test. It's called *test anxiety.*

Anxiety expresses fear, which is nature's way of keeping you out of trouble. Thousands and thousands of years ago, fear kept your ancestors alert. They watched carefully for any animals that might want to eat them. If they met a wolf, a bear, or a saber-toothed tiger, their heart would pound harder, which helped them run away faster.

Anxiety brings on quick action rather than deep thought. Not many ancient ancestors would have survived if they stood around thinking, "Hmm—that's interesting. This beast has much bigger teeth than the one that tried to eat me last week." The message of fear was: "Run for your life!" It shut down the thinking parts of the brain so those ancient people could fight desperately or make a fast getaway.

Today, fear still affects the body in the same way. However, during a test you don't want your brain to turn itself off while you run away. So feeling that anxiety can make it harder to think—and to remember all the facts you spent hours studying.

Now that you understand the physical part of test anxiety, you may still wonder what causes a person to feel fear about a test. After all, it's just paper—not a beast with big teeth. But some people see a test as a challenge that is as threatening as a beast. They set very high standards for themselves—or want to meet someone else's—to the point that they grow worried and fearful that they can't do well enough. Their anxiety about the test can allow their worst fear to take over. But there are ways to conquer that fear.

First, try the techniques suggested here. If you find that pre-test jitters are seriously getting in the way of preparing for exams, share your list of symptoms with your parents, your teacher, or a guidance counselor. If test anxiety becomes a serious problem, you may decide to seek help from a trained counselor or specialist.

Facing Test Anxiety

A *little* anxiety before a test is not a bad thing. It keeps you alert and on your toes. Everybody feels a little nervous going into a test. What you have to do is make sure your anxiety doesn't get in your way. To do that, you can take some steps before you even get to school.

For one thing, get plenty of rest. It's no good trying to pack facts into, or pull them out of, an exhausted brain. Lack of sleep makes you feel on edge, cranky, and easily frustrated. Once your feelings start to get out of control, you may become even more anxious.

In addition to getting a good night's sleep, leave plenty of time to get ready for school and to arrive early. Test days are not good times to arrive at the last minute feeling rushed and upset.

Eat intelligently for breakfast or lunch on test days. Try to have a healthy cereal (not Sugar Buzz Bombs) for breakfast. Eat a light meal for lunch, such as a simple sandwich and some fruit. You definitely want to stay away from fats, sugar, junk food, carbonated beverages, and spicy food. If test anxiety makes you feel strange, don't eat anything that can leave you feeling stranger. Eat food that gives you energy that lasts.

If you're allowed to choose your seat, pick one that's comfortable and away from open doors or other distractions. Now that you can prepare in the physical ways, also plan to make some mental preparations.

KEY 6

Put a stop to negative thoughts

There's an old story about a man who saved a magic elf. The elf gave the man a reward. He could have anything he wished for—as long as he could spend an hour not thinking about a purple elephant. The problem was, how could something as bizarre as a purple elephant *not* keep popping into his head?

Some students face the same problem with test anxiety. Negative thoughts can grow, with one thought leading to another one. It might start off with, "There's a hard test coming in two weeks." From there it goes to, "There's too much stuff to study." That leads to, "This is all too tough for me to understand," and that ends up with "I'm going to fail this test—big time." As these thoughts move along, they can become self-fulfilling predictions. Instead of studying, you worry. You can't sleep. You go to school jittery and nervous, convinced you're going to fail. By the time the test comes, you may be so rattled, you can't concentrate on what you did study.

How can you deal with negative thoughts when you're worrying about a big test? You might try to think about purple elephants instead, but there are more practical things you can do before and during a test.

The best advice for the weeks before the test is study, don't worry. Some people never get jobs finished because they get more concerned about how much they have to do instead of just doing it. If you set up a schedule for studying and stick to it, you have less time to get nervous. Also, the more you know, the more confidence you have when the time comes to face the test.

On the day of the test, don't spend much time talking about the exam with your classmates. The last 15 minutes before the test is too late for a group review, and listening to nervous friends can make anybody start thinking negative thoughts. Just make sure you get to the test early.

During the wait for the test papers to be passed out, everyone spends long minutes sitting at their desks. You have nowhere to go, nothing to distract you. Your brain may start to fill up with "what-ifs," and "Who's better?", and "Why couldn't I have been out sick today?"

This isn't the time to focus on useless worries or to go frantically thumbing through your textbook or class notes. Instead, close your eyes and try to call up an image of your study notes, or tune in a picture of the flashcards you've been using to study. What are the major facts you need for this test? Now is an excellent moment to gather them fresh in your mind. If this is a math test, ask yourself what formulas you'll need to use. By calling up these images, you're refreshing your memory about things you already know. You're programming your brain to start thinking about the material on the test instead of worrying about what's coming.

What should you think about during the test? The test questions and answers! Focus on one question at a time—don't worry about whether you can answer every question perfectly. It doesn't pay to take your mind off what you're doing to worry about how well you're doing it. And it won't help if you're busy wondering how *other* people are doing. This is *your* test. If other people finish early, pay no attention. Just continue working and do your best.

KEY 6

GETTING IT RIGHT

Have a conversation with yourself

If you talk out loud and have a conversation with yourself, some people might think you're a little strange. But having a few silent words with yourself is a perfectly normal thing to do. This method is called *positive self-talk*, and it can be a helpful tool for guiding your thoughts through a rough spot and helping you steer clear of negative thinking. Here's an example:

YOUR SCARED SELF: Oh, no! I can't do this! I'll never be good enough to get all these questions right.

YOU: What's the problem here?

YOUR SCARED SELF: This test—it's harder than I thought. I have to get a 100, and there's no way I can answer every question perfectly.

YOU: Slow down for a second! Now, of course you want to get a perfect score, but that's not essential. The important thing is to just get through the test today.

YOUR SCARED SELF: But it's got so many questions, and the paper looks so empty. And I don't think I know—

YOU: It's just an hour or so out of your life. You've been studying for two weeks now. Here's your chance to show off all that work. It's no big deal.

Become aware of your worries

Some people start to worry the moment a teacher starts talking about a test. Other people get nervous when they talk about the test with friends. Other people may lose their cool when they start thinking about how much studying they need to do. Still others start daydreaming about disasters when their notes and books are spread out in front of them and they're ready to start studying.

Do any of these people sound like you? What do you do? Becoming aware of how you react to tests—from the very first time you hear about one—can help you learn to control your thinking and responses about the test before worries start to build up. If you can identify when you *first* feel the fear, then you can start to handle those fearful thoughts before they have a chance to take hold of your imagination. One way to handle them is to use the positive self-talk technique just shown; another way is to learn to relax.

Ways to Relax

When you're going through test anxiety, relaxation is probably the last thing on your mind. However, you can learn to relax . . . with a little practice. Here are several ways to do it.

Breathing helps

During your conversation with yourself, you remembered to take a deep breath. Deep breathing *does* work to help calm you down. Controlling your breathing plays a part in activities as diverse as martial arts, yoga, sports, dance, and even dramatic performances.

If worries are getting on your nerves, sit down. Close your eyes and tell yourself, "Okay. Time to relax."

KEY 6

Take a deep breath. Bring the air in through your nose, and keep it coming until your lungs are completely full. Your chest and your stomach both go out because they are filled with air.

Hold that breath for a slow count of three. Then let all the air out through your mouth. Keep pushing until you can feel it emptying from your chest and stomach.

Try this deep-breathing trick two more times. Each time you inhale, remind yourself you're taking in calm. Each time you breathe out, you're blowing away stress and worry.

When you finish, open your eyes. Do you feel different? Some people suggest that deep breathing brings more oxygen into your system, which is healthy and refreshing. Also, it may be that controlling one set of muscles helps release tightness in all of them. However it works, many people are surprised at how much better they feel after those few deep breaths.

Tighten and loosen muscles

Another way to unlock your muscles is to sit down and close your eyes. Try to make the muscles in your face and head even tighter than they are. Strain at it. Know exactly how it feels. Then take a deep breath.

As you breathe out, consciously loosen up the muscles in your scalp and forehead . . . then in your face.

Now tighten the muscles in your neck and shoulders. Pull your shoulders up towards your ears as you breathe in. Release all that tension as you breathe out.

Concentrate on the muscles in your chest. Take a deep breath and tighten them, then loosen the muscles as you let the air out.

Clench your hands and arms with another inward breath. Breathe out and relax. Your arms should hang loosely beside you. Shake out your fingers.

Do the same tense-and-release trick with the muscles in your stomach as you breathe in and out. Clench and unclench the muscles in your thighs. Breathe in, breathe out. Tighten and relax the muscles in your lower legs. Finally, clench and relax the muscles in your feet and toes.

KEY 6

How do you feel—tighter or looser? Remember, this technique should be done while you're sitting down. It's a lot harder to do if you're standing or walking. If you try this technique lying down, you may get *too* relaxed. So don't take too long before you get back to work.

See which relaxation exercise works for you and keep practicing. When should you practice? Try it whenever you feel yourself getting tense over an upcoming test. If studying starts feeling too intense, take a short break and relax. If you start getting negative thoughts, use them as a reminder to start using your relaxation techniques.

Visualization techniques

Another way you can beat test anxiety is by *visualization*. With this method, you create a detailed mental image of what you want to accomplish. Most students admit that daydreaming is the biggest cause of lost studying time. Here's a chance to turn your daydreams to a useful purpose. In fact, try to make them as realistic as possible.

What sort of mental pictures should you create? Try this on for size. Close your eyes and use deep breathing to relax. Then "see" yourself really

It's a Test— Relax!

Many people use relaxation exercises during actual tests. Just remember, however, that full-fledged relaxation techniques take time, and time is always limited when it comes to tests. Rather than going whole-hog on a relaxation exercise, try to get by with a couple of deep breaths and a change of position in your seat.

concentrating as you study. Add as many details from your room as you can. You want to be able to feel the reality as you hit the books and take notes. Now open your eyes and get to work. The idea here is to make your daydream come true. You may surprise yourself with a more positive attitude. What your brain can imagine, your body can often do.

Better study habits lay the foundations for success. For test anxiety, the best mental image shows you being calm and confident while answering exam questions. Close your eyes and relax. Imagine the room where you'll take the test. Feel the pen in your fingers, the papers under your hand. Keep it realistic. Maybe you can skip a couple of questions, to come back to them later. You want to program your brain with the image of yourself working and making progress. The actual grade isn't so important—you're just trying to get yourself used to the idea of doing better.

Of course, you're not going to make this daydream come true just by wishing for it. You still need to work at studying and reviewing material. However, if you spend a couple of minutes a day visualizing success, eventually you can make it come true on test day. Spend a few minutes thinking how happy you'll feel at the end of a test you've just completed.

KEY
6

Ready, Set, *REVIEW*

1. Take a sheet of paper and write down how test anxiety affects you. Try to be as precise as possible, like a doctor listing symptoms. "I feel lousy whenever I think about tests" doesn't really tell much. "I get so upset over how much I have to read that I can't study" gives a lot more information, but you can make it even more precise. "I get really upset when I sit at my desk in my room and see how many pages I have to read. And I don't have enough time!" That presents the problem and also suggests a solution.

   To get started, answer these questions:
   - When do I get stressed out?
   - Are there any particular things that spark my test anxiety?
   - How do I feel when I think about taking a test in each of my classes?

2. Using your list to identify your most obvious trouble spots with test anxiety, write up a plan to do better. Where are the places where you can improve your preparation and your performance? Use the information in this chapter to find better ways for you to handle your anxiety. Then set goals for putting them in place.

IMPROVE WITH EXPERIENCE

✓ **Review Returned Tests**

✓ **When Your Scores Are Poor**

✓ **Building Self-Confidence**

> *Whether you're facing the football field, the ballet studio, or your desk, experience builds confidence. The more experiences you have, the better you will do.*

One way to improve is to look at past mistakes and work to improve them in the future. You can do that with tests by reviewing your previous tests. You also can take a closer look at your studying strategies and make a plan to intensify your efforts.

As you gain more experience with taking tests, you'll gain more and more confidence in yourself. This self-confidence has a domino effect—the more comfortable and capable you feel, the easier it becomes to handle the challenges that tests can bring your way. Before you know it, you'll be looking forward to taking on your next test!

Review Returned Tests

You can learn a lot from a returned test. This is where you find out how well you studied and how your test-taking strategies turned out.

Read all of your teacher's comments

If you're like most students, you just check the mark at the top of the test. Maybe you go over the grading to make sure the points come out right. What about those little notes in the margins, though? They are there to help you learn what to improve upon. Test comments are an important form of communication between you and your teacher. If you see "Very Good," you have a right to be proud. If you see "Needs More Work"—guess what? You have more work to do.

The important thing is not to let your feelings get in the way as you read comments. It's nice to get compliments and to see improvements your teacher may have pointed out, but you also have to be able to accept criticism. If the red marks on your test paper are pointing out mistakes, your teacher also may try to be helping you see the reason for those mistakes.

Reading your teacher's comments can point out specific problems you're having. With the help of your parents and your teacher, these comments can also lead to solutions. School problems don't necessarily have to be with class subjects. For example, a teacher once noticed that a student's math scores had suddenly gone down. Looking over the student's work, the teacher found that the math problems were actually worked out correctly. But the *numbers* in the problems weren't the

GETTING IT RIGHT

Does this test paper look like something you might see in your class? It shows typical questions, typical answers—and typical teacher comments.

You're making more of an effort, but more work is still needed.

Spelling

1. Pennsylvania was settled by ____Quackers____ led by William Penn.

Weren't you paying attention when we reviewed this?

2. Newfoundland was discovered by ___John___

3. _____ The Iroquois were know as the Seven Nations.

4. _____ Pierre La Salle claimed Louisiana for France.

5. The oldest city in the U.S. is

Did you miss these or not understand them?

   a. Boston
   b. New York
   c. Los Angeles
   (d.) St. Augustine

6. The ship that carried the Pilgrims was

This essay need more information. Did you understand this question? You describe Spanish colonies, but there is very little about the English colonies.

   a. The _Pinta_
   b. The _Mayflower_
   c. The _Golden Hind_
   d. The _Puritan_

7. Essay Question: Compare the Spanish and the English colonies in the New World.

There were many differences between English and Spanish colonies. Often the Spanish people who came to California and Florida came from Mexico. The English people came from England. The native people worked in missions in the Spanish colonies instead of importing slaves.

Missions were very important parts of the Spanish colonies. Besides teaching religion, they had ranches and farms. A lot of Native Americans worked at the missions. Governors were appointed in Mexico and worked for the Spanish Kingdom. There was less democracy.

KEY 7

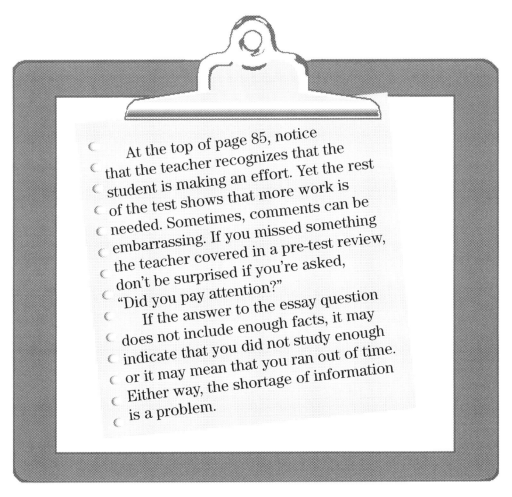

At the top of page 85, notice that the teacher recognizes that the student is making an effort. Yet the rest of the test shows that more work is needed. Sometimes, comments can be embarrassing. If you missed something the teacher covered in a pre-test review, don't be surprised if you're asked, "Did you pay attention?"

If the answer to the essay question does not include enough facts, it may indicate that you did not study enough or it may mean that you ran out of time. Either way, the shortage of information is a problem.

ones that had gone up on the blackboard. The difficulty wasn't the math—it was with the student's eyesight. That was taken care of, thanks to the teacher alerting the child's parents. The moral of the story? Sometimes teachers see more clearly than students do. When looking at a test paper a teacher can learn a lot about how you're doing.

What kinds of questions are your weakest?

In addition to looking to see what points you got on your test paper, you should be looking to see what got points taken off. Did one particular section receive lots of red ink?

Lots of incorrect answers on single-answer questions may mean you aren't preparing properly. Since that's the question type that depends on pure recall, if you can't remember the answers, something isn't working with your studying. Did you merely read through the material once, or did you make flashcards and review them often? Sometimes reading out loud or writing down answers can help set things in your memory.

Difficulties with true/false or multiple-choice questions may suggest a completely different problem. These are questions where you're supposed to recognize things you've studied. Besides taking a second look at the way you study, you may want to consider why you're picking wrong answers.

Why did you make mistakes?

As you go over your test for the questions you missed, try to remember why you chose each answer. Was this something you knew? If not, why didn't you know it? Did you skip a chapter you were supposed to study? Did you miss putting this information in your notes because you weren't in school? Or did you mistakenly put the wrong information in your notes, and study that?

Often, teachers devote a class to reviewing a recent test—yet many students don't understand why that's important and how it can benefit them. Actually, your teacher is giving you another chance to learn the correct answers. If the same question turns up on a midterm or final, do you want to miss it again because you never bothered to learn it?

Compare your answer to the correct one and try to see where you went wrong. Did you mess up on the instructions? Did you really know the answer, but latch onto a look-alike multiple-choice response and not look farther? Were you not reading questions thoroughly because you were rushed for time?

K
E
Y

7

Even when you weren't marked wrong, you might hear about a better answer during the test review. Make notes. Try to come up with ways you could improve. Most importantly, hold on to the test and those notes! Don't just toss them back into a notebook or folder, or stick them somewhere in your desk at home. You'll want both the questions and the answers on hand to guide you as you practice for the next test.

Learning from mistakes

A corrected test offers a pretty good road map for future exams—and for future study sessions. Look at the *way* questions are presented. Does your teacher use challenging words? Did you find a lot of double negatives, super-modifiers, and qualifiers in the true/false questions? What kind of answers turned up in the multiple-choice questions? Were there similar answers or very different ones?

Also notice what sort of directions appeared on the test. On the single-answer questions, were you supposed to write in the words from a word bank, or use the numbers or letters in front of them?

Still more important is the question of where the questions came from. If you recognized sentences from your textbook in many of the questions, next time hit that book a lot harder. That text should become your main source for study guides and flashcards. On the other hand, if you think more questions came out of class discussions, start listening closely. Learn to be more careful when you take class notes. Double-check the facts as you review to make sure you got things down correctly, and don't be afraid to ask questions in class if any points are unclear or give you difficulty.

As you look at more tests, you begin to learn what kind of answers your teacher likes. What's the exact word or phrase that's wanted for a single-answer question? What sort of language gets the best marks on

essays? Once you know the answers to these questions, you can tailor your answers to meet the teacher's expectations.

Another important thing to consider as you go back over a test is time. Did you use the test time wisely? Did you get hung up on a question or section and then exceed your time budget? Did you give in to test anxiety or get a bad case of "test-day daze?" Learning how to beat the clock is important. You can't prove your knowledge if you aren't able to get it down on the test paper in time.

Becoming test-smart means practicing how to take tests as well as practicing the material. Use a clock to see how long it takes you to handle homework. Break it down by types of questions. How much time do you need for single-answer questions? . . . for true/false? . . . for multiple-choice?

With a kitchen timer, you can then transform homework assignments into exciting games of "Beat the Clock." The idea is to get yourself used to turning in neat, correct answers quickly, just as you're supposed to do on a test.

If you work with a study group, you can get lots of practice questions. The group can even create practice tests, using returned test papers as a guide. Make up a time budget for the different test sections, set your trusty timer, and see how well you do.

When Your Scores Are Poor

Everybody—even the class brain—can mess up on a test or quiz. The important thing is the way you deal with it. If you just hide the test paper and lie low, you're not going to fix what's wrong. In fact, you're probably setting yourself up to fail the next test.

Remember, part of becoming self-confident means that you're always willing to learn. That's a particularly good attitude to have in school, since learning is your job. So, how does a bad test score help you to learn? Keep reading.

Identify your problem

Your test comes back with lots of red ink. Take a deep breath and start reading your teacher's comments. They may not be too pleasant, but if you're going to turn things around, you need all the help you can get.

All the things you've read in this key—checking comments, finding weak questions, understanding why you made mistakes—become more important when you've really done badly on a test. A poor grade means that something went seriously wrong with your preparation.

Was the test harder than you expected? Maybe you thought you could get away with less studying. In that case, a poor grade means you'll have to change your schedule to prepare for the next tough test. If you spent lots of time studying, then you have to look at how well that time was spent. Were there distractions around, like the TV, radio, or a younger brother or sister? Perhaps all that memory work—making flashcards and writing outlines—seemed like too much to do. A dismal test result shows that whatever you're doing just is not enough.

Now you have to play catch-up. If there's a review class on the test, work hard and pay serious attention. Get all the right answers and compare them to what you put on the test. What kinds of facts couldn't you come up with—the little details, the big picture, or both?

If a test shows you have real problems, don't let pride or shyness stand in the way. Use the returned test to

INSIDE SECRET

A poor grade can be a wake-up call

Perhaps you had been drifting along, not doing too badly. But now the first real test has shown just how unprepared you are. Here's a crucial clue—as you go through the test, do you find that you're already hazy about the answers you got correct? Is what you studied—facts, dates, vocabulary, or scientific processes—already fading from your memory? If so, you definitely tried to cram too much. The good news is that you still have time to turn things around.

KEY 7

identify the things that are difficult. Work up questions, and approach your teacher after class. Do it soon after the test, so the material is fresh and you can refer to the exam. You may get some special help, or you may not be the only one having a tough time. The whole class may need some special review. At the very least, you show that you're trying do better—and your teacher will see that.

One idea to consider is asking someone to work with you. Although a classmate might help, someone further removed might be a better choice. Many students dread the thought of working with a parent or think their parents don't want to be bothered. However, if you have serious concerns about getting your studying done, consider asking your parents or another adult to help. If you prefer to have only a certain type of help from them, try describing exactly what you want them to do and explain that you'd like to continue doing your other school-work on your own.

Make a plan of attack

You've gathered all the clues and have a good idea of what your problems are. Now you have to start working on the solution, which means you need a plan.

If test anxiety got in your way, review Key 6 on that subject and allow extra time in your study schedule for relaxation exercises and positive self-talk. If you try that and still have a problem, talk to your parents about scheduling a meeting with your teacher, who may able to help if he or she is aware of the problem—and don't wait until ten minutes before your next test!

Go over your studying methods with a critical eye. You've heard it before—research shows that repeatedly reviewing material over time helps you remember it better. That means that the longer information is in your brain, the better you'll remember it. Remember, you have more

tests in your future, including the final exam. Wouldn't it be easier—and less stressful—if you already know your facts when final exam time comes?

Put your plan into action

Hoping and intending to do better won't cut it. You need results, not promises. Making a plan means you know what you have to do. Now you have to follow your plan and do it.

Beating test anxiety won't happen in a day. You'll have to be on guard for stress and negative thoughts while you prepare for the next exam. Try the relaxation exercises and see if they work. Are you able to think more clearly and study better? If you suffer from severe test anxiety, find ways to chart your progress while you work on the problem. As you study more, your homework assignments and class participation should improve, clearly showing your teacher—and you—that things are turning around.

If you discover gaps in your test preparation, work out how to fill them. If you missed classes, borrow a friend's notes to make up for the lost work. Try to get the best notes you can. If these notes contain items that you don't understand, discuss them with your teacher to make sure you get them down clearly.

For textbook study, write down your assignments carefully. Make sure you're reading the right sections. After you read, make notes. Compare your notes with the text. Read them out loud. Does the material make sense to you? Discuss it with parents or classmates. If you need to, work up questions to ask your teacher.

Once you've made up a study schedule, stick to it. Get a rough estimate of how long it takes you to read a section and make notes about it. That can help with your schedule—and let you know when you're wasting time. The more you get used to regular review, the easier it is

K
E
Y

7

to do. As the next test comes near, you'll be happy to discover how much you already know—and how it makes test preparation a lot easier. (Appendix B at the end of this book has a Time Assessment Form and other tools to help you manage your study time.)

Homework sessions can help you train yourself in the art of reading questions carefully. Examine your textbook questions—even the ones you don't have to do. Compare them to questions that confused you on old tests. How are they alike? How are they different? As you go through new material, invent test questions of your own. Word them like the questions that confused you. That way, you come to recognize similar questions in the future.

To get additional practice, pretend that some of your homework assignments are tests. Time yourself while you take them, "grade" them yourself by checking your textbook and notes to double-check your answers, and pay close attention to any anxiety you may feel. In this way, you have additional opportunities to handle time management, review information, and deal with anxiety.

Whatever your test problem may be, you can improve if you examine the problem, make a plan, and work at it. Each test you take tells you whether you're succeeding, or whether your plan or your work needs some tweaking.

Building Self-Confidence

Self-confidence means looking at yourself in a positive, yet realistic way. It means you can see your strong points and your weak points, and that you know how to handle yourself. It means aiming for your best and sticking up for yourself, but being able to take criticism.

What can you do to build confidence in yourself? How can you encourage yourself to have more positive thoughts and keep calm when you face challenges? Give these suggestions a try!

- Don't nag yourself with doubts and criticism. If you've prepared well for a test, you can expect to succeed.

- Set realistic goals. If you're failing a course, don't try to force yourself to get a perfect 100 points on the next test. Getting a passing grade may be the best you can do right now. If you do even better, you have a right to be pleased. Life is a journey, and you make it step by step.

- Always keep learning. If you don't succeed, don't beat yourself up. Find out why you had trouble. If you fail a test, talk with your parents and your teacher. Where did you go wrong? What do you have to change to meet your goals? Do you need a new plan? Will it take more time than you expected to accomplish what's needed?

- Take responsibility if things don't go well—and take credit when they do. Don't downplay real achievements by saying you were just lucky.

- Concentrate on your strengths, not your weaknesses. It can help to keep a list of past successes to remind yourself of your achievements. Again, be realistic. For instance, if you want to do better in Social Studies because that's not one of your strong subjects, that's no reason to run yourself down. Remind yourself that you are good at Math—and you can apply the same determination to do well in other subjects.

Just about every week on TV, some sports team shows how attitude makes the difference between winning and losing. When you go into any situation—especially tests—thinking you're going to fail, you may create a self-fulfilling prediction. If you go in prepared and ready to do your best, you'll soon see yourself succeed.

K
E
Y
7

Ready, Set, *REVIEW*

1. You've got an old test hidden somewhere. Maybe it's tucked behind the cover of your notebook. Maybe it's crumpled in the bottom of your book bag. Dig it out and start looking for clues. Could you come up with correct answers now for the questions you got wrong? Do you still understand the answers for the questions you got right? If this test were given tomorrow, would you do better or worse than the mark you have now? A test can tell you a lot about where you stand in a class.

2. How well did you really read this key? Find out by answering the following five questions. Find the most complete answer among the four choices.

   1. Graded tests should be
      A. kept private.
      B. fought over for every possible point.
      C. used to find clues for improving.
      D. shown to your parents.

   2. After-test review classes allow students to
      A. get back into the swing of class work.
      B. rest after cramming for an exam.
      C. talk to their teacher about test anxiety.
      D. learn how to correct what they got wrong.

   3. When studying for a test, the most important thing is
      A. how many hours you spent working.
      B. reviewing all your notes and materials consistently over time.
      C. taking good class notes.
      D. reading the textbook.

4. When you've gathered the clues to your test problem
   A. you should get professional help.
   B. you should carefully read your textbook.
   C. your parents should complain to the teacher.
   D. you should make a plan to improve.
5. When you make a plan to overcome test problems
   A. make a schedule that fits into family plans and activities.
   B. cover every little detail.
   C. follow through and chart your success.
   D. show it to your teacher.

ANSWERS:
1. C
2. D
3. B
4. D
5. C

KEY 7

APPENDIX A

Standardized Tests:
A Sample of What You're Expected to Know

Today, educators across the country track how students are doing with statewide or national tests. Some school districts give these standardized tests to every student at every grade level. Other districts test at specific intervals, such as the fourth- and eighth-grade levels.

On the next few pages, you can see sample questions in the subjects of Reading, Science, Math, and Social Studies. This gives you an idea of what a standardized test looks like for upper grade levels of elementary school. You also can see if these are the kinds of questions you can handle.

To answer most standardized tests, you must fill in a bubble form. Use the sample bubble form provided here and try it out as you answer the following questions. An answer key appears at the end of this appendix.

Reading	Science	Social Studies
1 Ⓐ Ⓑ Ⓒ Ⓓ	4 Ⓐ Ⓑ Ⓒ Ⓓ	7 Ⓐ Ⓑ Ⓒ Ⓓ
2 Ⓐ Ⓑ Ⓒ Ⓓ	5 Ⓐ Ⓑ Ⓒ Ⓓ	8 Ⓐ Ⓑ Ⓒ Ⓓ
3 Ⓐ Ⓑ Ⓒ Ⓓ	6 Ⓐ Ⓑ Ⓒ Ⓓ	9 Ⓐ Ⓑ Ⓒ Ⓓ

Reading

Read the following selection and answer the questions that come after it.
All questions have only one correct answer, so choose the best one.

Broadway—more than a street

For most people, "Broadway" brings images of glamour, stars, and musical shows. "The Great White Way" is the center for live theater in New York City—and America. Yet the theater district, with all its glitz and glamor, is only about half a mile long. Broadway stretches more than 13 miles from one end of Manhattan Island to the other. It crosses by bridge into the Bronx and extends up into Westchester County. There it becomes a highway continuing to Albany, more than a hundred miles away.

On a map, Broadway seems a very willful road. It cuts diagonally across the square grid of Manhattan streets, causing traffic jams at every intersection. But then, the New York City street plan came along only in 1811. Broadway was there centuries before.

Few people know that this celebrated city street started out as a Native American warpath. Four centuries ago, Manhattan was inhabited only in summertime. Nearby tribes set up camps for hunting and fishing. Parties of warriors moved along the path that became Broadway to raid rivals.

After 1624, Broadway became a trade route. Natives carried furs down the road to the Dutch colony town of New Amsterdam. As years went by the road became a cow path. Cattle moved north among farms to go to pasture. They moved south to be sold in New York City.

As the city grew, Broadway's wandering ways became a problem. The government began buying land to straighten Broadway. However, corrupt deals were discovered. This scandal led to the downfall of the legendary Boss Tweed.

Today, Broadway moves past skyscraper business buildings, giant department stores, and favorite theaters. It also runs along tree-lined blocks, holding together a city that never sleeps.

1. Broadway is most famous for:
   A. Being disobedient
   B. Creating traffic jams
   C. Being very long
   D. Being the home to many theaters

2. Native Americans traveled along Broadway to
   A. Get cattle
   B. Attack New Amsterdam
   C. Buy land
   D. Raid their enemies

3. What does it mean when Broadway is described as a celebrated city street?
   A. The street is very wide.
   B. The street is very famous
   C. The street has many parades.
   D. Many stars walk on this street.

Reading

1 Ⓐ Ⓑ Ⓒ Ⓓ
2 Ⓐ Ⓑ Ⓒ Ⓓ
3 Ⓐ Ⓑ Ⓒ Ⓓ

Science

Read the selection below and answer the questions that come after it. All questions have only one correct answer, so choose the best one.

Liquid	Solid	Gas
Honey	Meat	Steam
Water vapor	Diamond	Oxygen
Mercury	Ice cube	Carbon Dioxide

4. Which item is placed under the wrong heading?
   A. honey
   B. water vapor
   C. meat
   D. carbon dioxide

5. Which group correctly shows a food chain?
   A. mouse < clover < snake < horned owl
   B. clover < mouse < snake < horned owl
   C. clover < snake < mouse < horned owl
   D. mouse < snake < clover < horned owl

6. Each year, the Earth moves once around
   A. The Sun
   B. The Moon
   C. The stars
   D. Its axis

Science

4 Ⓐ Ⓑ Ⓒ Ⓓ

5 Ⓐ Ⓑ Ⓒ Ⓓ

6 Ⓐ Ⓑ Ⓒ Ⓓ

Social Studies

Read the selection below and answer the questions that come after it.
All questions have only one correct answer, so choose the best one.

7. The first Europeans to settle in Canada were:

   A. Quakers

   B. French

   C. Puritans

   D. Portuguese

Social Studies

7 Ⓐ Ⓑ Ⓒ Ⓓ

8 Ⓐ Ⓑ Ⓒ Ⓓ

9 Ⓐ Ⓑ Ⓒ Ⓓ

8. Which is the source of this quotation? "We hold these truths to be self-evident; that all men are created equal, that they are endowed by their creator with certain unalienable rights, that among these are life, liberty, and the pursuit of happiness."

   A. Patrick Henry's Speech to the Virginia Convention

   B. The Declaration of Independence

   C. The Presidential Oath of Office

   D. The Preamble to the Constitution

9. A carpenter builds a desk for the doctor who cured his wife's illness. Which word best describes this exchange?

   A. Barter

   B. Tariff

   C. Auction

   D. Favors

Mathematics:

Answer the following questions.

10.   8.3

     X 5.7

     _____

11. Write the following number in standard form: fifteen billion, four hundred forty-seven million, seven hundred sixty-eight thousand, twenty-three _____

Answer Key

1. D
2. D
3. B
4. B
5. B
6. A
7. B
8. B
9. A
10. 47.31
11. 15,447,768,023

APPENDIX B

Scheduling Your Time for Prime Studying

Time Assessment Form

To begin with, you have to take an honest look at how you spend your time. Take a typical week and chart it on the Time Assessment Form on the next page. Write down how many hours you spend on various activities. Add them all up, and then subtract the total from 168—that's the number of hours in a week. How much time do you have left over? How do you use it?

Setting Up Your Schedule

Are you surprised to see how you spend your time? Was there an activity that took up a lot more time than you expected? Did that please you? What takes up the most time? What takes up the least? How does studying fit in? Would more study time improve your grades?

The easiest way to get control of your time is to make a schedule. Just don't get too detailed—you don't need to schedule when to take every breath, but you do need to *prioritize*. That means to break down your life according to what's important. Look at it this way. There are things you must do, things you should do, and things you'd like to do. Must-do things affect the way you live—like going to school, studying, or sleeping. Tidying up your room or going to sports practice are things you should do. Hanging out with friends and watching TV are things you'd like to do. Must-do things always bump less important items. Give important jobs plenty of time, and don't crowd them on your schedule.

Time Assessment Form

What I do	How long it takes
Homework	
Get ready for school	
Go to classes	
Work, chores, errands	
Sports/after school activities	
Get to and from school	
Family activities	
Enjoy friends and leisure time	
Watch television	
Play video/computer games	
Shopping	
Eat meals	
Sleep	

Are there any other special activities that take up your time?
For instance, do you spend time at church? Go to the doctor or
dentist? Take piano or dancing lessons? Do you have a hobby?
Fill them in below:

TOTAL	

Hours of the week minus your total:

168 - _____ = _____

Time Assessment Chart

	Sun.	Mon.	Tues.	Wed.	Thurs.	Fri.	Sat.
6:00 A.M.							
7:00 A.M.							
8:00 A.M.							
9:00 A.M.							
10:00 A.M.							
11:00 A.M.							
12:00 P.M.							
1:00 P.M.							
2:00 P.M.							
3:00 P.M.							
4:00 P.M.							
5:00 P.M.							
6:00 P.M.							
7:00 P.M.							
8:00 P.M.							
9:00 P.M.							
10:00 P.M.							
11:00 P.M.							
12:00 A.M.							
1:00 A.M.							
2:00 A.M.							
3:00 A.M.							
4:00 A.M.							
5:00 A.M.							

APPENDIX C

Top Ten Tips for Remembering What You Studied

In recent years, scientists have studied how the brain receives and remembers information. That's the good news. The bad news is that the kind of facts usually found in textbooks is the most difficult information for a brain to store. Still worse, they've discovered short-term memory begins to fade quickly. You start forgetting most of what you learned in the first hour after a class.

This means that you can't rely on facts just "sticking." You have to make an effort to get material you need for tests into your long-term memory. The following tips offer some basic points that can help the brain function at its best during test-taking times.

1. **Decide that you're going to remember.**
2. **Decide what to remember.**
3. **Break information into chunks that are easier to remember.**
4. **Review before you read.**
5. **Read to remember.**
6. **Learn how you learn.**
7. **Say it.**
8. **See it.**
9. **Go long, but keep study sessions short.**
10. **Review, review, review.**

INDEX